MW01002280

From the Ashes

By Gina Russo

with Paul Lonardo

INFINITY
PUBLISHING

ISBN 0-7414-5791-1

Published by:

INFI(∞)ITY
PUBLISHING.COM
*1094 New DeHaven Street, Suite 100
West Conshohocken, PA 19428-2713
Info@buybooksontheweb.com
www.buybooksontheweb.com
Toll-free (877) BUY BOOK
Local Phone (610) 941-9999
Fax (610) 941-9959*

Printed in the United States of America

Published September 2010

This book is dedicated to all those who were affected by the tragedy of the February 20, 2003 Station Nightclub Fire, the families and friends of the victims, the survivors and in particular the one hundred people who lost their lives:

Louis S. Alves, Kevin Anderson, Stacie Angers, Christopher Arruda, Eugene Avilez, Tina Ayer, Karla Bagtaz, Mary H. Baker, Thomas Barnett, Laureen Beauchaine, Steven Thomas Blom, William Christopher Bonardi, Kristine Carbone, Richard A. Cabral, Jr., William Cartwright, Edward B. Corbet III, Michael Cordier, Alfred Crisostomi, Robert Croteau, Lisa D'Andrea, Matthew P. Darby, Dina Ann DeMaio, Albert Anthony DiBonaventura, Christina DiRienzo, Kevin J. Dunn, Lori K. Durante, Edward Ervanian, Thomas Fleming, Rachael K. Florio-DePietro, Mark A. Fontaine, Daniel Frederickson, Michael Fresolo, James Gahan, Melvin Gerfin, Laura Gillet, Charline Elaine Gingras-Fick, Michael James Gonsalves, James Gooden, Derek Gray, Scott C. Greene, Scott Griffith, Pamela Gruttadauria, Bonnie L. Hamelin, Jude Henault, Andrew Hoban, Abbie L. Hoisington, Michael Hoogasian, Sandy Hoogasian, Carlton "Bud" Howorth III, Eric James Hyer, Derek Brian Johnson, Lisa Kelly, Tracy F. King, Michael Joseph Kulz, Keith Lapierre, Dale Latulippe, Stephen M. Libera, John Longiaru, Ty Longley, Andrea Mancini, Keith A. Mancini, Steven Mancini, Judith Manzo, Thomas Marion Jr., Jeffery Martin, Tammy Mattera-Housa, Kristen McQuarrie, Thomas Medeiros, Samuel Miceli, Donna M. Mitchell, Leigh Moreau, Ryan M. Morin, Jason Morton, Beth Mosczynski, Katherine O'Donnell, Nicholas O'Neill, Matthew James Pickett, Carlos L. Pimental, Sr., Christopher Prouty, Jeffrey Rader, Teresa Rakoski, Robert L. Reisner III., Walter Rich, Donald Roderiques, Tracey Romanoff, Joseph Rossi, Bridget Sanetti, Rebecca "Becky" Shaw, Mitchell Shubert, Dennis Smith, Victor Stark, Benjamin Suffoletto, Linda Suffoletto, Shawn Sweet, Jason Sylvester, Sarah Jane Telgarsky, Kelly Viera, Kevin Washburn, Everett "Tommy" Woodmansee, Robert Daniel Young.

FOREWORD

It has taken time for me to come to this realization, but I believe that the fire happened for a reason. And I'm not talking about cause or responsibility, but something more elemental. I'm talking about consequence. I'm talking about personal destination. I don't claim to fully understand all the reasons, and for each survivor it may be different, but for me I know that one of the reasons was to bring some of the people I've met since the fire into my life. Of course, I wish the fire had never happened for innumerable reasons. But it did happen. And nothing is going to change that now. However, the friendships I've made as a result of the fire have made a world of difference for me in my recovery. It was largely due to these relationships that I was able to find the strength and courage within myself to overcome my injuries and personal loss and continue on with my life. This is what this book is all about.

You saw the list of names on the previous pages of the one hundred people who lost their lives in The Station Nightclub Fire. That list stops far short of naming all the people who were physically and emotionally scarred by the flames, individuals whose lives have been significantly alerted as a result of what happened in a small, otherwise unexceptional nightclub in West Warwick, R. I. on a cold February night in 2003.

I can't begin to tell all their stories, but if by sharing my own story I might inspire someone who believes they have lost everything to take a closer look at what they *do* have, then they, too, might find hope and happiness despite their personal misfortune. Coping with any life-changing tragedy is difficult. Adjusting to those changes is a process, sometimes a lengthy one. Like planting a seed in soil, it may not seem like a whole lot is happening at first, but a life rebuilding itself needs time to grow. When it does, then that person, in turn, might inspire another to make something positive out of something that seems utterly bleak.

I can only say from my own experience that I feel I owe certain people a debt of gratitude that I can never repay. Not only for what they did for me, but for what they showed me I can do for myself. I can't imagine life without them now. These people have been a source of strength, support and inspiration for me. At the same time, it made me realize who my true friends really were. This understanding sometimes came as a surprise, as people you thought would be by your side were not. Other times, I was surprised to find that some people I hadn't seen in years, friends from high school or earlier, and sometimes complete strangers, have since become some of my closest friends. As for my family, we have always been close, and this event only brought us even closer together. Their love continues to be a source of strength that I draw from on a daily basis, and without the presence of my mother, stepfather, sister, brother, brother-in-law and my children, I would not have come out of this ordeal the way I did. To all of them, as well as the doctors, healthcare workers, fire fighters and the innumerable individuals who gave their time, money and prayers to us all, I thank deeply.

-Gina Russo

From the ashes
of that which you were
You return--
The memories remain,
The fire still alive
And this is how, ablaze,
You return
Into that which was
My existence
From the fire
Of that which you were made
You return, The memories return
You speak to me
And now, ablaze
Love returns
To that which was
Our life
From the fire
Of that which we were
You return--
The memories die,
Love fades away
And now, smoldering
You return
To that which you once were
whole again.

--Unknown Author

CHAPTER 1   ANATOMY OF A DISASTER

The small nightclub was rocking like it never had before. The wait staff was busy and the bar was doing a brisk business. The aggressive advertising and promotions for the live metal venue seemed to pay off as streams of people continued to pour inside to listen to the music and have a good time. By all accounts, it was a big success. And the headlining band hadn't even taken the stage yet. Jeffrey Derderian, one of the club owners, was on hand to observe the high energy and robust crowd, and the only problem he might have foreseen was not having enough stock of a particular bottle or draft beer.

Jeffrey Derderian was also a television news reporter for a local CBS affiliate, WPRI-TV Channel 12 in Providence. Brian Butler, a cameraman for Channel 12, was there with him to shoot footage for a story the news station was doing on public building safety, ironically enough. Just four days earlier, a stampede at a nightclub in Chicago had claimed 21 lives. The idea was to show a local club that was up to code and safe.

Being featured on a report concerning property in which he owned was a clear conflict of interest, but that oversight would be the least of his worries this night. He co-owned the club with his brother, Michael, who was in Florida on this particular night.

Outside the nightclub, the working class neighborhood of West Warwick, Rhode Island was getting ready for bed, watching the local news on television and waiting for *The Tonight Show* to come on, undisturbed by the thunderous riffs from the opening acts playing at The Station nightclub. Even the closest neighbors could scarcely hear the heavy metal music because it had been effectively muted by a thick layer of low-density polyurethane foam that lined not only the walls and ceiling around the stage, but extended out further into the interior of the club, all the way to the rest rooms across the main room.

In June of 2000, shortly after ownership of the facility changed hands, the eggshell-like packing foam was installed with the authorization of club management. Following repeated police complaints by neighbors that the music was too loud and disturbed them when they tried to sleep late at night, the foam was an inexpensive solution to a potentially serious problem, which if it had not been promptly remedied could have cost the club its liquor license. The only problem was that the thousands of square feet of foam that had been glued to the walls and ceiling was never intended by its manufacturers to be used as soundproofing material. It worked well enough to that end, all right, but it was not suited for interior use because the material was not fire retardant. It is normally used in packaging and product display. The low ignition rate and high flame spread rate of the foam was what made it so dangerous. Not only that, but if introduced to flame this material would unleash a host of toxic chemicals, including deadly cyanide gas. Much safer, flame retardant acoustical-dampening material would only have cost about two times the price of this stuff.

By the time the second act, Trip, was finishing up their set, over four hundred people were packed inside the 4,500 square foot single-story wooden frame building. Two hundred fifty-eight was the listed capacity limit, but club owners this night figured they could easily squeeze in 317 people, which was the highest occupancy limit for a public facility, set by the city of West Warwick around the time the current club owners took over. By removing the pool tables, vending and other game machines from the main floor and lining them up in front of the "greenhouse" windows at the front of the club, they created additional open space for people to stand while they watched the concert.

No one willing to purchase a ticket for the show was turned away that night as fans from a dozen states turned out to listen to the music of Great White, a Los Angeles-based rock group whose success peaked in the late 1980's. In 1990, Great White was nominated for a Grammy for best hard rock performance for "Once Bitten, Twice Shy," their biggest hit. Now, more than thirteen years later, and long after their fifteen minutes of fame had expired, two sadly ironic lines from this song would live forever. From this night forward, whenever this title track would be sung live or played on the radio, these lyrics took on a completely different meaning from when they were written.

...You didn't know that rock-n-roll burned
So you bought a candle and you lived and you learned...

Just after 10:30 p.m., Trip completed their final set and left the stage. A popular local heavy metal DJ, Michael "Doctor Metal" Gonsalves, promptly jumped up on stage and began tossing WHJY souvenir T-shirts and hats into the crowd. His radio station was not a sponsor of the concert that night, but they did promote the event, in which Gonsalves, also referred to as "The Doctor," was emceeing.

Anticipation was running high as everyone waited for Great White to take the stage. It was 11:07 when "The Doctor" finally introduced the band. The house lights suddenly dimmed, and after a moment a set of multi-colored strobes were illuminated, washing over the members of Great White who were now in their positions on the raised platform acting as a stage. The audience cheered and clapped, an exuberant welcome for the faded rock stars.

No one inside the club at that moment could comprehend what was about to unfold. Nearly a hundred people did not know that they had less than two minutes to live. Their fates were permanently sealed in the next instant when Daniel Biechele, the band's tour manager, turned a key that simultaneously triggered three pyrotechnic devices, known as "gerbs." The foot long tube-like structures had been set up along the walls in front of the drummer's alcove, a recessed area at the back of the stage where the drummer sat. These fireworks began to spew plumes of brilliant sparks all the way up to the low ceiling. It made for a great entrance and added to the crowd's excitement.

At the same instant, the music started and lead singer Jack Russell suddenly appeared. As he began to strut his middle age stuff across the stage, he spoke briefly to the audience. His greeting barely audible over the raucous crowd, and then he launched right into the opening number, a song called "Desert Moon."

"Let's shake this town, Baby..." Russell screamed into the microphone.

Behind him, the pyrotechnic display continued, three dazzling fountains of light and heat that delighted the crowd. For seventeen seconds they showered to floor and ceiling with bright, white hot embers. Before they were through, however, the sparks ignite the

2 ½ inch thick foam on either side of the alcove. The left side started to catch fire immediately, then nine seconds later flames appeared on the wall on right side of the platform.

Television cameraman Brain Butler had his lens trained on the stage as the fire erupted. Among the images captured, many patrons were clearly seen holding their positions, watching the glowing flames, either believing it was all part of the show or expecting the fire to be quickly extinguished.

Great White's tour manager immediately knew that something wasn't right as he saw the sparks become flames. "I think I'm in trouble," Daniel Biechele said. "I fucked up."

Ten seconds after ignition, Jack Russell also realized that something was wrong. He could be heard on tape, saying, "Wow!...This ain't good!" He made a vain attempt to douse the flames with the contents of a water bottle. But the fire continued to spread and Russell and the band played on. Sixteen seconds after the fire started the flames reached the ceiling. A moment after this happened, Brian Butler started to retreat toward the exit, his camera never wavering from the fire spectacle at the back of the band's platform.

Paul Vanner, The Station's sound technician and stage manager, was standing on one side of the stage and witnessed the eruption of the pyrotechnics. He had a clear view as the shower of sparks touched off two separate fires along the walls on either side of the drummer's alcove. Even before Jack Russell dumped the contents of his water bottle on the blazing foam, Vanner moved quickly toward the rear of the club, where he retrieved the only working fire extinguisher, which he knew was mounted on the sound board.

"We got a serious fire issue," he said as he passed by the band's sound engineer. Vanner tested the extinguisher as he returned to the stage, but even in the short period of time that it took him to complete this round trip, mere seconds, he saw to his shock and horror that the fire was already burning out of control. The extinguisher he was carrying would have had as much effect on the flames now as Jack Russell's water had a few seconds earlier.

The highly combustible material in the soundproofing foam acted as an accelerator, enhancing the speed and intensity of the flames, at once devouring more and more precious oxygen and emitting dense black smoke that blinded, choked and poisoned.

It took twenty-five seconds for the flames to reach the ceiling on the left side of the platform, now the walls and ceiling on both sides of the alcove were ablaze. Underneath the foam that was being misused as soundproofing, the main ceiling consisted of drop foam panels, which were not as combustible or as toxic as the packing foam, but the panels were not flame retardant, either, and caught fire easily enough.

At this point, most people seemed to realize that this was not part of the show, and en masse started to back away from the stage and shuffle uneasily toward the exits. Some moved more quickly perhaps than others, but did not rush. Others, however, held their ground, listening to the music and watching the fire, perhaps disbelieving what they were seeing. Or entranced by it.

At thirty-seconds, Great White suddenly stopped playing and the band members began to jump off the stage like rats fleeing a sinking ship. All but one escaped through the nearby stage door.

By now, everyone recognized the potential danger of the situation and proceeded with more urgency toward the front door.

At thirty-six seconds, the first cell phone calls were received by the state's 911 call center reporting a fire at The Station. It was 11:09 p.m. The information was relayed to West Warwick's fire dispatcher, who initiated a standard structure fire response. Emergency response units initially dispatched to the scene included four engine companies, a tower-ladder truck and a Battalion Chief from the West Warwick Fire Department.

Precious seconds were passing, but as each one ticked away time slowed immeasurably to everyone trying to evacuate the burning nightclub.

At about forty-one seconds, the heat detector/fire alarm system went off automatically, activating a shrill alarm and accompanying strobe lights. There was no sprinkler system in place because this safety precaution was not even required by state law until 2003, and previously existing facilities such as The Station were "grandfathered," or exempt from complying because the building had been erected before the law took effect.

The evacuation continued in rather orderly fashion during all this. Then the lights suddenly flickered off, and that changed everything. Panic gripped the crowd as they were plunged into instant darkness. Suffocating clouds of black smoke gathered and banked down close to the floor, making it impossible for patrons to see where they were or anyone they may have been with. Terrified, those still inside blindly pushed and shoved their way forward, rushing in the direction where they thought the front door might have been, starting a bottleneck that slowed escape drastically.

Looking at the front entrance from outside the burning building, it might have appeared that the fire was spitting out one or two people at a time, as if from the jaws of some mythical beast, breathing out black smoke around each as they emerged.

Most people inside were not aware that there were alternative exits, three others besides the main entrance. There was a single door off the main bar and an exit from the kitchen. Both of these were on the left side of the building, beyond the crush of bodies converging in the center of building, and they would not have been easy to locate even if access to them had not been blocked. The kitchen was walled off from the main function rooms and by now all illuminated EXIT signs guiding patrons to external doors would have been completely obscured by the suffocating blanket of smoke. There was also a single door on the opposite side of the building just to the right of the stage that opened up onto a small lot where the band's bus was parked. This would have been the quickest and easiest means of escape, but a person would have to know it was there and they would also have to completely ignore a natural survival instinct by heading straight into the path of the fire.

Though some managed to find these other exits and escape, about two-thirds of the patrons attempted to get out through the doors at the main entrance. In most cases of sudden evacuation, people will seek to exit through the same door that they had entered.

With this route impassable, however, some people decided to take their chances and find another way out, heading indiscriminately out in all different directions. A few mistakenly wandered into the rest rooms at the back of the club, where no doors or windows existed. The windows in an adjacent office were barred. These areas became death traps, and anyone caught in them was quickly overwhelmed by the toxic smoke and gas filling the building.

It was just one minute after ignition and the fire had spread all the way across the ceiling of the dance floor, thirty-three feet from the stage, where many people were trapped and clambering desperately over one another to get to the front door. With the dense cloud of toxic Black Death bearing down on them, the fleeing patrons encountered an "L" shaped wall with a ticket-taking booth which funneled everyone into a smaller and smaller space. Hundreds of people were trying to get out through this three-foot wide egress. If they were fortunate enough to make it that far and squeeze through this tight spot they would have reached a set of swinging doors which opened up into an entrance hall. From there, it was still another fifteen feet to the double entrance doors and safety beyond. After fifty-four seconds, Cameraman Brian Butler reaches the entrance lobby, the camera rolling. He made it safely outside at a minute and eleven seconds after the fire began, but did not stop filming.

Jeffrey Derderian also escaped unharmed. He was seen by several witnesses securing the small cash register containing the receipts for the evening from a club employee. Of everything that could have been lost that night, and had been lost that night, a wad of cash was all he thought to save from the flames that were rampaging through the building and everyone inside.

After a minute and twenty-six seconds, about half of the crowd had escaped with their lives by this point, but the remaining people were still inside the burning building. In order to escape this hellish nightmare, people inside began to bust through the glass of the greenhouse-like windows at the front of the building, as well as the front windows of the main barroom on the other side of the club. This action saved many lives, but it also supplied the fire with an endless source of fresh oxygen, and as heavy black smoke rolled out of the building, the flames inside grew even stronger and hotter. This was plainly visible from outside looking into the club through the stage door.

At the seat of the conflagration, the combustion gases from the burning debris were already at the lethal stage, and the extreme temperatures and heat fluxes of the fire were well within excess of accepted survivability limits. For anyone who may have been thinking that breathing the air closest to the floor would buy them some time, they were mistaken. The air down there was just as lethal. Anyone breathing this air would have quickly succumbed, inhaling deadly superheated gases.

The area around the stage was first to become fully involved in fire, scorching the air to a temperature in excess of 1,200 degrees, and climbing steadily. It became so hot that anything combustible ignited. The structure was composed mainly of dry wood whose construction dated back to World War II. The building material acted as kindling, and the tar paper used simply liquefied and melted, raining down on the escaping patrons like black lava. This "flashover" effect set not only the surrounding walls and ceiling ablaze, but clothing and hair spontaneously burst into flames, scorching flesh whether it had been covered or exposed. The smell of burnt hair and flesh permeated the air. Anyone not near an open door or broken window, where there was access to fresh air, would have already perished by now.

Close to the entrance, those who were overcome by smoke inhalation fell to the ground unconscious. Still others, conscious but disoriented from oxygen-deprivation, fell or were pushed to the floor and were unable to get back to their feet. This human stampede continued to push forward, up and over the fallen, in many instances pinning them where they lay, including in the very threshold of the front doors. Some were trapped under the crush of bodies all around and on top of them and could not move. At a minute forty-two seconds, Butler focused his camera lens on the front entrance to capture disturbing images of people inexorably wedged in the doorway and screaming for help as smoke poured out around them. For some, escape may have been just an arms-length away but they were doomed as the grim pile of bodies quickly rose until the exit became constricted entirely.

It was about a hundred seconds after the pyrotechnics triggered the fire, and no more patrons would pass through the front doors on their own.

Outside, some of those who had escaped, many with minor injuries and burns of their own, became the first rescuers, pulling people outside through the broken windows and from the pile at the front door.

The building continued to burn, and after three minutes the interior was completely engulfed in flame.

Station #4 of the West Warwick Fire Department was less than a half mile away on Cowesett Avenue, and the first fire engine arrived about four minutes after the initial 911 call was placed, well within the limit of the NFPA standard for fire department response. However, the loss of life that can occur in a fire rampaging for four minutes can be catastrophic.

Rescue workers arrived at the scene and were greeted by a grim tableau of devastation and human suffering. As experienced as any individual fire fighters may had been, some were shocked to see that flames had already begun to break through the roof. Before the first line had been dragged to the scene or a single drop of water was evaporated by the heat, a large column of fire blossomed above the building and rose up into the night sky.

People were running around the parking lot, some were on fire. They tumbled on the ground to put the flames out, sometimes assisted by other people, some covered with blood from deep lacerations from broken glass. A few burn victims could be seen diving into snow banks to soothe and cool their scorched flesh. Several victims in an obvious state of panic began climbing onto the fire trucks and other rescue vehicles as they arrived, begging to be helped.

It was complete chaos.

The emergency workers' first task was to contain the injured for treatment, which was made all the more difficult because some people were leaving the scene, just getting into their cars and driving away. Others were wandering around in a state of shock among the parked cars and into the surrounding woods. The number of injured were numerous and each survivor they encountered was worse than the next. If these were the people that had escaped, God help anybody that was still inside, they thought.

At 11:13 p.m., five minutes after the fire started, flames were observed extending out of the front door and the broken windows. Fire fighters were in a race against time as they tried frantically to dislodge as many people as they could from the pile at the front entrance, grabbing arms and legs indiscriminately, pulling the ones they could to safety. Some people were feebly reaching their arms out, moaning softly, or unable to call for help because of the crushing weight of the dead and dying against their chests and abdomens. Their clothes were on fire. They were being burnt alive. Others were not moving at all, crushed to death or smothered even before the smoke and flames could harm them. The clothes of some of the victims were burned off completely and the charred skin sometimes slipped off the limbs in the hands of the rescuers as they tugged, making the task difficult and gruesome.

A 1 ¾ inch hose line had been dragged near the front door and water from the booster tank on Engine 4 was initiated at 11:14 p.m. About six minutes after the deadly fire was ignited, the first drops of water touched the flames. Over the pleas of the suffering all around them, fire fighters began dosing the front entrance with water, including the bodies of the living and dead stacked in the threshold like human cordwood. Some of the hoses were being pinched by cars and emergency vehicles coming and going from the scene, diminishing the precious flow of water to little more than a trickle at times.

Battalion 1 quickly activated the Warwick Task Force, which invoked a mutual aid agreement and seven additional engine/ladder companies from surrounding communities were dispatched to the scene. At that time, Battalion 1 also requested twelve ambulance units.

At approximately 11:22 p.m., Warwick Fire Chief Jack Chartier responded to the scene. The severity of the situation prompted him to ask the fire dispatcher to contact Metro Fire Control and implement the Mass Casualty Incident Plan, which would call rescue vehicles from all around the state to descend upon the West Warwick blaze. It would also put area hospitals on alert for massive casualties.

Soon after this, a general alarm went up, ordering all personnel to evacuate the structure. It was just moments before portions of the roof and walls came crashing down. When this happened, rescue workers knew it was over, as temperatures inside would have reached upwards of 2,000 degrees, the standard temperature at which human remains are reduced to ashes in a crematorium. Suddenly the mission of fire fighters switched from a rescue operation to one of recovering bodies, as more and more of the victims pulled out were turning out to be lifeless. In order to preserve the human remains and aid the coroner's office in identification of the bodies, they still had to put out the rampaging fire.

Miraculously, the combined rescue efforts resulted in nearly one hundred unconscious and barely conscious people being pulled out of the burning building.

Some fire fighters on scene were injured after attempting to enter the inferno to rescue any remaining survivors or to douse the flames closer to the seat of the fire. The intense heat melted the tar on the roof, and a molten rain dripped down all around them.

Fire Chaplains busied themselves praying for the dead and dying on the scene. An emergency makeshift triage area was setup in the parking lot of the Cowesett Inn across the street.

Ambulances were departing to area hospitals with multiple victims on board. There simply were not enough vehicles to accommodate the numbered of injured, despite efforts of multiple municipal rescue squads and private ambulance companies from around Rhode Island and Massachusetts. RIPTA buses were used as shuttles to transport victims who were not as badly injured. Fifteen different hospitals received wounded. Kent County Memorial in Warwick was nearest to the disaster, and received a majority of the victims initially. Victims with the most extensive burns were transported directly from the scene by helicopter to regional burn centers, including Massachusetts General and Shriners Hospital for Children, which specializes in burn care.

At about 11:57 p.m., a main section of the nightclub roof collapsed. The fire chief immediately ordered a roll call to account for all fire fighters on the fire ground. All were present. Then shortly before midnight, the Warwick ladder unit raised its ladder and began applying a master stream to the center of the fire. Up until then, the master streams had been directed by fire company Engines and concentrated on the flames closest to the front entrance, where many bodies of victims and survivors were first observed. A master stream is a fire service term for a water stream of 350 or more (up to 2,000) gallons per minute. This kind of water pressure is too great for hand line use and is delivered by devices called a fire monitor, a high-capacity water jet that can be aimed and controllable with great degree of ease. Most apparatus-mounted fire monitors can be directed by a single firefighter, compared to a standard fire hose which normally requires several.

Fifteen minutes later, another portion of the roof, above the sun room, near the front of the nightclub, suddenly collapsed.

By 1:00 a.m. on February 21, 2003, the State Fire Marshal was on the scene. The incident commander asked the fire dispatcher to cancel additional rescue units, while Triage reported that all the patients had been transported from the scene.

Ninety minutes after ignition, the ambulances stopped coming. They were no longer needed. Hearses began to arrive instead. The smell of burnt flesh hung in the air and red stains in the snow was a grim testament to the massive loss of life that had occurred there. The temporary medical triage center at the nearby Crowne Plaza Hotel had been replaced by grief counseling services.

The fire had been extinguished. There was almost nothing left of The Station nightclub. It was a smoldering husk, which a couple hours before had been filled with close to five hundred people. How many had died, or would die as a result of their injuries from the fire, was not precisely known at that time. Those who had been on scene and assisted in the rescue effort knew the number would be high. Giving some indication of the exorbitant loss of life was the parking lot and the neatly lined rows of cars that would never be driven by their owners.

The scene was crowded now with state officials, investigators and the media.

As word of the fire spread, concerned family and friends also began to converge on the scene of the disaster, as well as area hospitals to learn of the status of their loved ones.

Rescuers and investigators worked through the night, sifting through the rubble for remains and personal belongings that might help identify victims. Powerful floodlights were brought in to illuminate the disaster scene. A green tarp was erected to shield the carnage from the eyes of the curious public.

By daylight, the bodies of victims were still being recovered, many of them found in clusters. It was apparent to investigators that most never made it more than a few feet from where they were standing when the fire erupted, succumbing almost instantly to the heavy smoke and toxic gases. Very little of the structure remained intact. The only recognizable feature was the piece of wall along the left wing and, paradoxically, a portion of the drummer's alcove where the fire originated.

Late the next morning, heavy equipment was called in to sift carefully through the heavier pockets of debris of what remained of The Station. As these excavating machines did their grim work and more clusters of charred bodies were uncovered, the death toll continued to rise steadily. Positively identifying the remains was the foremost challenge facing authorities at that time.

The Federal Disaster Medical Assistance team was activated and they called in five teams of pathologists who worked around the clock for several days to assist in identifying the remains of the victims. 90% of the fatalities could not be identified without DNA and other forensic and pathological methods of detection. The federal Disaster Mortuary Operational Response Team (DMORT) was also called, lending a team of twenty-five experts, including forensic pathologists and dentists, X-ray technicians, as well as other technical and support personnel. Many other federal and state agencies became involved, and all of them worked together, making identification a top priority.

Summoned soon after the fire to lend their expertise to the investigation were two renowned international experts in their respective fields. Forensic scientist, Henry Lee, who headed up the Connecticut State Police forensic science unit as well as the Henry C. Lee Institute of Forensic Science at the University of New Haven, also in Connecticut, lent his formidable detection skills, as did John DeHaan, a revered criminologist and fire expert. Lee has given expert testimony in many high-profile and celebrity criminal homicide trials, including the O. J. Simpson murder case. DeHaan, author of a widely studied textbook on the scientific study of fire, came to Rhode Island with thirty years of practical experience at fire and explosion sites around the world at the request of personal injury attorney, Mark Mandell.

From the beginning, the prime focus of the investigation became the highly flammable polyurethane foam that had been adhered to large portions of the club's interior walls and ceiling. The chemical composition of the foam was important for many reasons, including how it affected the spread rate of the fire as well as the toxins released when it combusts.

It is known that smoke inhalation is the leading cause of death in a fire, upwards of 90% of all fire-related fatalities, in fact. Typically, most people do not burn to death because smoke inhalation usually occurs first. This is the breathing in of any number of suffocating and toxic gases, most of which is carbon monoxide. Because our blood is chemically more inclined to bond with this colorless, odorless poisonous gas than it is to oxygen, it makes any combustible material extremely hazardous. Carbon monoxide not only poisons body cells, tissue and organs, but it removes life-sustaining oxygen and you suffocate.

It was understood from the outset that there was going to be a maximum effort to find out what happened and why not only to learn from this tragedy and take the necessary measures to ensure that such a set of circumstances would never again conspire to kill and maim so many people needlessly, but also to gather enough evidence so that the guilty and negligent were punished.

Ninety-six people had perished that night and early the following morning. Upwards of two hundred survivors had suffered burns and various injuries, including seventy-four who required hospitalization. Nearly two dozen of these were in critical condition, clinging tenuously to life, a portent that the death toll would rise, which of course it did.

After all the victims had been recovered and the evidence collected, much it removed from the site for closer study and inspection, almost nothing remained of the structure that once stood there. But to many, the site became an instant memorial. By the weekend after the fire, thousands of people made a pilgrimage to the site of the disaster, many in chartered buses. Family and friends gathered there in support of one another. Every face was slackened in disbelief and anguish. The steady, soaking rain may have masked the tears, but not the emotion as people consoled one another in front of the blackened footprint of The Station nightclub.

It was reported that this catastrophe was the single worst disaster to strike the state of Rhode Island since the Great Hurricane of 1938, which claimed the lives of 262 people. Nationally, The Station Nightclub Fire became the fourth deadliest fire in U.S. history.

CHAPTER 2   BEFORE THE FIRE

I grew up in a section of Cranston, Rhode Island known as Oaklawn Village. My family relocated to this small historical community before I was born. Like many second-generation Italian-Americans who lived in Providence, my parents wanted to get out of the city and settle in a suburb to raise their children. It was just my brother, Jim, until I came along on October 18, 1967.

Almost immediately, fire touched my life.

On Christmas Eve that year, our house burnt down. Fortunately, when the fire started, we were at my maternal grandmother's house in Providence celebrating the holiday in typical Italian-American family fashion. It was loud. There was too much food. The kids were screaming. The adults were joking and laughing. At the end of the night, when we were returning home we were passed by a fire truck at an intersection. My mother felt an instant of panic, and then looking up she noticed smoke rising in the distance. As my father drove closer, he realized the roads leading to our house were blocked off. He pulled around a rescue vehicle and saw the engine parked in front of our house. Fire fighters were dousing the flames. Some of the neighbors were watching the spectacle in their robes and pajamas from their windows or out on their lawns. Our car was stopped by a police officer and my father was unable to do anything more than what the neighbors were doing, watching our house burn.

Apparently someone had robbed us and, intentionally or not, started the fire because they were using matches instead of turning on the lights. The thief may as well have been *The Grinch* himself. The act instantly deprived my brother and me of our Christmas gifts that year, and of much greater consequence created a temporary inconvenience for my entire family.

While no one was hurt, the house did not fair nearly as well. The damage was so severe that we had to stay with relatives for several months while the house was repaired.

In a rather ominous bit of foreshadow, my parents were later told that when the fire fighters first arrived, they didn't know if anyone was home and entered the burning house to conduct a search. One rescuer noticed my bassinet, empty and scorched, in my parent's bedroom. He immediately became concerned that a child may have been inside, and searched the entire house looking for me.

Only two months old at the time, I obviously have no memory of this event, but this was not the first time that my family experienced personal tragedy with fire.

Going back further, to 1945, my maternal grandmother's uncle, his two children and two grandsons were killed in a tenement fire in Providence. They were sleeping when an electrical fire broke out while they slept. They children went to bed and never woke up.

It sometimes makes me wonder if this was my destiny all along. Could fire be a personal plague that runs in our family the way cancer and other afflictions do in others?

Growing up, however, there was no indication of any such predisposition. My childhood was a pleasant one, despite being the middle child. Besides an older brother, I have a sister, Stephanie, who is three years younger than me and my best friend. The three of us have always been close, even as adults, but my sister and I did everything together.

My mom, Carol, came from a big family, one of four sisters. So I had plenty of cousins, some of whom I am very close with to this day. We all grew up together and they became my friends. My maternal grandmother was like a second mother to me. She was always there for me and I knew I could count on her for anything.

I didn't know my dad's parents. They died before I was born. My father's name was James, but everyone called him Jack, which was his middle name. He worked hard as a foreman at Colonial Knife Company and provided us with everything we needed. We went on family vacations every summer to Hampton Beach, New Hampshire as far back as I can remember. Some of my best childhood memories are from those trips.

Unfortunately, health problems hindered my father throughout his life. At the age of 32 he had been diagnosed with diabetes and then seven years later he survived a severe heart attack. Doctors did not expect him to survive. This was quite a contrast to the health status of the relatives on my mother's side of the family, where my grandmother lived to the ripe old age of 92.

I attended local schools, Oaklawn Elementary, Western Hills Middle School and Cranston High School West, graduating in 1985. My senior year, the school helped me get a job working part-time at Rhode Island Hospital as a secretary. The position was only mine for as long as I was in school. However, after I graduated I wanted to stay on at the hospital, so the department where I was working created a position for me so I could continue to work there. And I jumped at it. My goal in life had always been to go on to nursing school. I didn't feel as though I was quite ready for nursing school at the time, so I thought it would be best for me to get as much work experience as I could in the mean time. Rhode Island Hospital has always been an excellent teaching hospital in every aspect, for nurses, residents and interns alike. I knew I could gain a lot of knowledge anywhere in the facility. Besides, I really liked the work and the people. I just wanted to be in the medical field. I truly loved it. It's something I thrived on.

I stayed in the same department for several years until I figured that I had learned everything I was going to learn there. What I wanted to do at that point was to work with patients, so I applied for a position in the Adult Outpatient Clinic Services Department, first as a receptionist. It was a great experience, and I met some amazing and interesting people of all kinds.

As my father began losing his battle with diabetes, he lost a toe due to the disease. Soon after this his doctor told him that he would have to go on dialysis before too long. Renal failure was inescapable, but he passed away in March 1987 at the age of 52.

During this time I was engaged to my first husband, James Odsen, who I married the following year, in August 1988. It was a difficult time for me, and looking back I believe that I rushed into the marriage and didn't take the time to really consider this step because my mind was preoccupied.

My Father's death changed all our lives, especially my mom's. She had known this man since she was fourteen and married him at seventeen, two weeks after graduating from high school. For ten years they had been unable to conceive a child, and had actually been in the final stages of adoption when my mom became pregnant with my brother. After struggling for so long to start a family of her own, within four years she had three of us.

My mom had worked part-time at local outlet stores while we were growing up, but after my father died a friend suggested she apply for a job at the Providence Gas Company where she worked nights. It would at least get her out of the house when she was most lonely. She was hired and this was where she met a widower, Vincent Richards, a man she would later marry, in 1990. I couldn't ask for a better step father. He's a great guy, who has always been good to my mom. They are still together today.

Around the time my first son was born in 1993, I began to feel a need for another professional change, more of shift, really, so that I could work with children. I was able to transfer into the Pediatrics Services Department, doing the exact same thing I was doing with Adults. And this is where I've been ever since. I knew when I started there that I would never want to do anything else.

My two sons and the children I worked with at the hospital everyday were the only things I lived for. My marriage was not working, and Alex and Nicholas and my job kept my mind off it. When we headed down the path to divorce no one was surprised, except James. He made the dissolution of this union as difficult and harrowing for me as he had made the marriage. I didn't know it at the time, but the relationship was doomed even before our children were born.

Alex and Nicholas, our two sons who came from this union, are true gifts that I wouldn't trade for anything. But I got married much too young, and I stayed with James longer than I should have. I met him when I was sixteen and was married at twenty. In that time, we went through our share of breakups but we always found our way back to one another.

Once we were married, I learned quickly that Jim was never going to contribute 50-50 to the relationship, but I foolishly believed I could make it work. We had different ideas of what life should be and where we were going. Of all the marital woes, Jim's emotional distance and his sudden lashing out at me for little or no reason was the most difficult for me to take. Money also became an issue and a source of many arguments. He would work occasionally when it was convenient for him, while I was holding down two jobs so we could make ends meet and try to save a little for the future. I stuck it out, and then five years into the marriage, Alexander James Odsen was born.

I thought having a child would have a profound impact on Jim, and that the responsibility would make him realize that everything was not just about him anymore. Well, I suppose he did come to this realization, but it wasn't to his liking. It was more than he could handle, and as a result he became more withdrawn, angrier when confronted. He completely stopped socializing with family and friends and would just go off on his own instead.

It was a very difficult period of my life, but I was thankful to have the family that I did because I don't know what I would have done without them. My parents watched Alex while I worked because Jim was never there. We separated a few times during our marriage, but I always fell for whatever story or excuse he gave me. He would apologize and I would take him back.

When Nicholas was born three years after Alex, I was thrilled that they would always have each other as brothers and friends their whole life. I was also saddened, though not surprised, when I realized that Jim was not going to be involved in the raising of these two beautiful little boys.

I will say this, I always believed Jim was a good father because as the babies got a little bigger he would take them for walks and play ball with them. He does love his children but he could never fully get himself to be a true family man, and this was the only way he ever harmed them.

For Jim and me, things only got worse. In fact, it became a nightmare. I got to the point where I just had enough of the struggling, the arguments and verbal abuse so I asked for a divorce in 1999. At first Jim mildly resisted the notion of a final separation, blaming me for all the problems we were having and proclaiming his innocence. He thought he knew me, and that I didn't really mean it or perhaps I was just fishing for another apology. When he realized that I was serious, however, he took this as a declaration of war and brought out the heavy artillery. The fighting became more intense, sometimes violent and involved the police on occasion. I was scared not only for me, but for Alex and Nicholas, and not because I thought their father would hurt them, but that something would happen to me and they would be without their mother. I got through it with the help of family and friends, and I stuck to my guns to see the divorce through to the end. It was the best thing for all of us. The paperwork wasn't finalized until July 2001, and when the ink on those signatures dried I felt like a great weight has been lifted off my chest.

After it was over, Jim resented me and my family and he did everything he could to make my life as difficult as possible. I've always thought that if he had put that much thought and energy into making the marriage work instead of trying to destroy every bond we once shared, then we would have had a healthy and happy relationship.

Looking back, I may have been naive, some would say blind, but I did love Jim and I'm not the kind of person to just give up on something.

In the years since the divorce, we can finally talk to each other. I do feel bad that he does not have a very good relationship with his sons but that is his doing and not something I feel the need to fix.

Despite the problems Jim and I had, perhaps even because of it, Alex and Nicholas have remained close. For young boys, they've been through quite a bit together, and seeing their father's behavior firsthand gave them an insight into how *not* to treat the people you love. He did not foster in our children the same sexist attitudes toward women that he possessed. The boys were smart enough not believe what their father had been telling them about me. They retained their father's name, but that was all, as they lived with me at my mom's and stepfather's house.

With all of that misery finally behind me, I began to look forward to the future and the possibilities it held for me and my family. I was happy being alone with my boys, but I wasn't soured on men. I wasn't about to blame all men for how Jim treated me during our marriage. I would like to have shared my life with someone special. I wasn't actively looking, but my eyes were open. Then on, May 2, 2002, I met a man who changed my life forever.

A couple months prior, on a lark and at the urging of a friend, Trish, we joined Hip-Dates.Com, an on-line dating service. She told me that I was not going to meet a nice guy at a bar. She was probably right, and I certainly wasn't going to meet anyone staying home every night.

But a dating service? I questioned myself.

It was not something I would have done on my own, but Trish talked me into it and afterward I couldn't believe that I had actually gone through with it. I certainly wasn't expecting much to come of it. I created a personal profile, as required, and thought that would be the end of it. However, I wound up getting several responses early on and I went on a couple of dates. I tried to keep an open mind and just have a good time. I hadn't been divorced all that long and I really needed to get out and meet new people. It didn't take long, however, to decide that this wasn't for me. At least it didn't seem to me to be any better of an alternative than meeting someone in a bar or club.

I realize that everyone has their strengths and weaknesses with different qualities to offer, and I do not believe that anyone, including myself, is better than anyone else. That said, you hope to find someone you can relate to on many levels, and I hadn't been able to find that with this dating service. It was on April 28th, after my last date had taken a bus to meet me at a Providence restaurant for dinner that I decided to remove my name and profile from the site once and for all. I was going to do it right after my date that night, in fact, but then I saw that I had gotten another response from someone. I considered ignoring the message, or even deleting it, and was strongly leaning in that direction, but for whatever reason I opened it and read through his profile. It was from a guy named Fred Crisostomi. He was a Navy veteran who owned his own painting company. He had posted a picture of himself with his two children and it was something that really jumped out at me. It wasn't the only thing, either. We had a lot in common.

I know it sounds corny, but it was truly uncanny how our interests were not just similar, but virtually identical. It was as if he'd copied my profile word for word. He liked all the same TV shows I did, the same movies, the same music and bands. He didn't smoke and detested the habit as I did. He just seemed like a really nice guy, and I just had to meet him.

As I was reading his profile, he logged on and we began to communicate to one another on the computer through an instant message feature. After about two hours of this, we broke one of the cardinal rules of the dating service by talking on the phone when Fred asked if I would call him. He said we seemed to be making a connection but the computer was getting in the way. I waited until my sons went to bed and then I called. We spoke for a long time, and I was not at all surprised when I learned that we knew some of the same people. In a state as small as Rhode Island, where everyone seems to know everyone, this is not unusual at all. The degree of separation is much smaller here than anywhere else in the country.

Still, when Fred told me that he had grown up in Silver Lake, I could not help but laugh when it turned out that it was the same Providence neighborhood as my ex-husband, whom Fred had been acquainted to some extent. It was not like they were best friends or anything, but growing up they had played in various youth sports leagues together.

In the same conversation, I discovered that our own paths had crossed, as well.

Fred had been talking about a particular basketball game that he played, and listening to him describe it, I realized that I had been there myself. So I was sure that we both had been at the same place at the same time, even if we didn't even know it. I wondered if maybe we had brushed by each other in the crowd that night, or if either of us had seen each other from afar, perhaps even making brief eye contact.

I even found out that I had known Fred's sister, Nancy, whom I had met through a girl my brother used to date. Crystal, his other sister, worked for the doctor that I was going to at the time. It was unbelievable. I looked at all these things as a sign that we were meant to be together. After only one phone conversation, I agree this was more than a bit of indulgence, pie-in-the-sky logic, but that's how I felt. I could hardly wait to meet him.

Meeting someone too soon was especially frowned upon, but we arranged to do that as well before we hung up that first night. It seemed unreasonable to both of us to have to wait only for the sake of waiting. We really wanted to meet one another, so a couple days later we did.

I was very nervous, but the instant I saw him in person I could tell that he was someone special. Then he gave me a big hug, which I loved. It was something I was used to coming from a big Italian family. We had just met, but I felt I knew him already. He was a genuinely nice guy. Sincere. And funny. He had a gentle nature that was obvious, and from the beginning he was better to me than any man had ever been, better than I ever thought anyone could be. And based on how I felt about myself from previous relationships, better than I thought I had deserved. Up until that point, anyway.

After the date, my mom was still up when I got home. She was about to ask me how my date went, but then realized she didn't have to after seeing the look on my face. The look on my face told her what she wanted to know. I was already thinking that this was going to be the person I would be spending the rest of my life with. The feeling that he might be "the one" was immediate, and over time my instincts were proven accurate. Fred felt it, too. The first thing he did when he got home from our date was call his sister. He told her pretty much the same thing that the look on my face told my mother.

The connection was that strong between us, and we spent just about every day together after that. Right up until the fire.

Because we both shared a strong passion for music, we went to many concerts in the nine months we shared. But we did a lot of other things together, as well. In September, we took a trip to Las Vegas with another couple. We also vacationed together with our children.

Fred was a fantastic father. He had a son, Brandon, who was nine then, and a stepdaughter Nicole, 13. From the start, we had both been anxious for our kids to meet. For two people who've just met, pushing to meet each other's children may not always be the best thing to do, and we probably could have waited, but it was as if we knew we only had a short amount of time together and we wanted to make every second count.

He treated my boys like they were his own sons. He was so much fun to be around and they responded to him. Alex and Nicholas adored him. Everybody did. He enjoyed life so much, and he reminded me that there was still so much for me to enjoy, as well.

The one thing about Fred that I was most drawn to was probably his unfaltering optimism. He was only thirty-eight years old when he died, but in the Crisostomi family there was a history of dying young. He knew this, and I think that had a major influence on his personality and why he had such a positive outlook on life. He tried to live healthy so he could get the most out of life, but he also wanted to enjoy himself. His sister, whom he had called to share his excitement the night of our first date, would tragically die a few years after Fred, also at the age of thirty-eight, when a heart attack would claim her life.

I had always considered myself a positive person, so I strongly identified with his outlook on life. We both preferred to interact as little as possible with people who give off a lot of negative energy. I know this makes my marriage to someone like Jim a complete contradiction to who I am as a person. For this reason, our union was the very definition of incompatibility. For far too long, even after the divorce, I didn't think I could do any better than Jim, and it really wasn't until I met Fred that I finally became convinced that I did deserve better.

For those who only knew Fred casually, his upbeat personality may have been most obvious in his love of sports. He had an extensive personal catalogue of sports memorabilia and collectibles. Everything from trading cards to signed jerseys and photographs. He was a big Yankees fan. In the winter, it was all about the New York Jets. But whether his team was winning or losing, on top or the bottom, he would always be smiling. This immutable hopeful nature, however, carried over into all aspects of life. Without exception, Fred was the most optimistic person I've ever met. No matter how bad a situation might be, he was able to find some good in it.

When my ex-husband expressed strong disapproval of my new relationship, I got scared, because I didn't know what he would do. Jim made me feel bad about myself for my strong feelings for Fred and for meeting someone on online though a dating service. Fred stood by me and told me it was going to be all right and I believed him. He made me feel safe and secure all the time.

It wasn't just me. Lots of people were drawn to Fred. He would do anything for you. He helped my step father paint the kitchen and dining room and refused to accept anything for it. His painting business was a success not because he was the best businessman, but because he was an exceptional person. His work was equally as exceptional, and he was very highly recommended by all his clients. Everyone loved him and he was always busy. He was getting too much work for him to keep up with, actually. But he would never even think of turning anyone down.

It was incredible to be around him. I feel fortunate for the time we had together. He taught me so much. About life. About myself. There's so much about him that I miss.

I want the world to know how special this man was and how special he will always be to anyone who was blessed to have been in his company. I owe my life to him. He still gives me strength today, especially on the darkest of days. I know he's there for me.

CHAPTER 3   FEBRUARY 20, 2003

Every Thursday night was family night at our house. My mother would cook a big pasta dinner and she would have everyone over. Sometimes there would be 15-20 people there.

I had taken that day off to spend some time with my kids. It was school vacation week, and since it had just snowed a couple days earlier, I thought it would be fun to take them sledding. My sister and her two boys, Dylan and Ryan, joined us at nearby Cranston High School West. It was cold, but we had a great time riding plastic sleds down the snow-covered hills that afternoon.

We did things like that together all the time, whether it was rollerblading, bowling or some other activity. It was always something. Our kids were close with their cousins, just as we had been with our extended family growing up. There is nothing like the closeness of a big family.

Fred had to work late, but the rest of us gathered for a big dinner that evening. I did what I could to help my mother prepare the meal, though in her kitchen she was in charge and did not usually dole out responsibility very easily. When it came to food or anything in the kitchen, it was her domain entirely. But I mixed the salad and set the table. It was a lot of work, but having everyone together made it all worthwhile. And next Thursday, we would do it all over again.

Fred joined us later, coming alone without his kids, who sometimes joined us. His son was being punished for something that night and his daughter was with her mom. The other kids missed Brandon and Nicole, but it was okay because Fred and I had plans to go to New Hampshire that weekend with our kids and they were really looking forward to it.

I remember Fred was in a great mood that night. He arrived wearing his work clothes and smelling of paint. I could smell him coming a mile away, and I knew he was there before I even saw him. He got out of his truck and spotted Alex and Nicholas. He immediately initiated a snowball fight. I heard the commotion and went outside. I laughed, seeing my three boys playing together.

A neighbor waved to Fred and she asked how he was doing.

"What a great day to be alive," he said, dodging a snowball.

It didn't seem like much at the time, but I'll never forget those words.

A ceasefire was eventually declared and everyone came inside to dry off and have some coffee and dessert.

After everyone left that night, Fred and I were hoping for a night out alone before our trip up north. I asked my parents if they would watch Alex and Nicholas for a few hours. My mom agreed, so now all we had to do was decide what we were going to do. We quickly agreed on a movie and rushed to the theater, but when we got there we found that it already started. We didn't want to miss the whole beginning and we didn't want to see anything else so we drove to his house to regroup and try to come up with alternate plan.

It was around 9 p.m. when Fred went online to see if there was anything interesting happening that night. That's when he opened an e-mail link from The Station, a local rock-and-roll club that we had been to together a number of times. When he saw that Great White was playing there that night he asked me if I would be interested in going to the concert.

I hesitated. I wasn't a big fan of the group. Plus, we didn't have tickets. And because it was getting late, I told him I thought it might be better if we just stayed in. He didn't seem to be disappointed, so we just sat down on the couch and started to watch TV. Flipping through the stations, there wasn't a whole lot that interested us.

Around 10 p.m., Fred turned to me and asked again about seeing Great White at The Station. Before I could say anything he called The Station to see if the concert was sold out and was surprised to hear that there were still people coming in. When he learned that Great White wasn't going on until eleven, I could see that he was starting to get really excited. Seeing Fred's enthusiasm, there was no way I could let him down.

Of all the clubs we had been to together to listen to live music, The Station was probably the one that we visited the least. The last time we had been there was to see *Human Clay*, a Creed tribute band, who were breaking up and performing together for the last time in the area.

In the nine months we spent together, we had been to some great concerts, as well as a few not so good ones and everything in between. From Journey, one of my all-time favorites bands, to a Rick James concert. REO Speedwagon to Alice In Chains. Tesla was a band that Fred and I really enjoyed seeing perform. I had already been familiar with their music, but Fred was the one who reintroduced me to them, and they've had a major influence on my life ever since, not just as a fan, after establishing personal relationships with some of the band members.

Considering the musical gamut we'd experienced together, I thought to myself, *what the heck, why not Great White?*

I told Fred if we were going to get there on time, we'd have to leave right away, and we would only stay for a little while. Fred immediately called his cousin, Rene Valcourt, who he facetiously called *Ugly*, because Rene was actually quite handsome. He got his cousin's voice mail and left a message for him.

"Hey, Ugly," Fred said. "We're going to The Station tonight to see Great White if you want to come meet us. But we're not going to stay long."

At 10:30 p.m. we walked out the door. Fred's house was just down the street from the club, just a couple minutes drive. We got there with time to spare, so we stopped at the bar to order a drink from Julie Melini. It was a quarter to eleven then because I remember someone asking Fred what time it was as we were standing there and he was paying for the drinks.

Then we began heading closer to the stage to get a good spot to watch the show. There were definitely a lot of people inside The Station that night, but strangely there was plenty of room to move around easily or stand comfortably. Along the way, we stopped briefly to chat with a few friends before winding up right in front of the stage. I remember saying hello to Linda Fisher who was selling merchandise for the bands. Fred went to the men's room and when he got back Doctor Metal was tossing WHJY caps and shirts into the crowd. We were standing so close that he just reached down and handed me a T-shirt and Fred a hat.

The excitement of the crowd had slowly been building. You could sense it. The energy level at any concert always ramps up just before the featured act comes on. It was really high that night, which was remarkable for such a small venue.

It was after 11:00 p.m. when Great White was introduced and the band came out. Jack Russell screamed something that I couldn't hear over the crowd noise and the band took up their instruments, launching right into their opening song.

As fireworks went off behind Russell, a roar rose from the crowd and it was hard not to get caught up in the excitement.

Fred recognized right away that something was wrong with the fireworks even before there was any fire. He pointed it out to me, gesturing toward the displays. They were throwing out a lot of sparks and it didn't seem as if they were ever going to stop. A moment later, the first flames appeared.

"Look," Fred said to me. "The walls are on fire."

He didn't say anything more. He just grabbed me firmly by the shoulders as flames began to work their way up the walls around the drummer's alcove. I put my drink down on the stage, right beside the feet of Jack Russell, who was singing as if nothing was wrong. Most of the audience appeared equally unconcerned as Fred guided me to a door along the right side of the stage, just a few paces from where we were standing. We were immediately confronted by a bouncer, who stepped in front of us and prevented us from leaving the building.

"We need to get out right now," Fred said.

The bouncer held his ground and shook his head. "Not this way. This door is for the band only. Club policy."

The man repeated this mantra after Fred yelled that there was a fire and the building needed to be evacuated. The bouncer may not have been aware of the flames, positioned as he was around the corner from the alcove, his view obstructed by a wall of speakers, but he did not believe us, either. I don't know if he thought we were making all this up in order to become stowaways on the band's bus out back, but he would not take us at our word, remaining adamant about not letting us pass.

Fred was incensed, to say the least, by this man's behavior. It was a pivotal moment beyond anything he could ever have imagined at that point. Just a few feet away from Fred was the rest of his life, but this very large man was standing in our way. What would have become of both of us had we gotten through the door at that moment is hard to say, but we certainly would have not been numbered among the victims or casualties of the horrific fire that hell was giving birth to behind us.

Fred was not a violent person, but if he had known that getting through that door would have been the difference between life and death, he would have found a way to get by, or through the colossus standing in our way. But Fred could not see even one minute into the future. He only wanted to get me out of the club before it went up in flames, and he thought there was more time. He had no way of knowing just how fast-moving this fire would be when he turned to me and said, "We can't stay here and argue with this guy. We have to get out of here."

Fred believed it would be faster to just make our way to the front door and escape that way. We had experienced no resistance, after all, getting inside and moving through the crowd a few moments earlier.

Fred turned away from the bouncer and wrapped both his hands around one of my wrists, pulling me with him through the club.

As we moved forward, we passed people who were dancing and singing along with the music, even with the alcove now visibly on fire. They could only have thought that it was all part of the show. The smoke was dark and had nowhere to go, so it began to fill the room. It was inconceivable that anyone would delay exiting the building, and I didn't think to say anything to them as I was whisked past them.

With the stage engulfed in flame and the fire continuing to advance quickly across the ceiling, the band suddenly stopped playing. It seemed that everyone became aware that their lives were in danger all at once. The sound of shattering cocktail glasses and beer bottles could be heard all around. There was no panic. People just dropped their drinks and moved quickly away from the fire. Almost all of them headed toward the front door.

Then the lights went out and the screams and shrieks of terror precipitated a stampede, snaring Fred and I in the middle of it. The crowd, which had seemed so sparse and navigable just moments before, congealed at once and our progress slowed to a near stop. It was pitch black. I was coughing from the smoke. Everyone was body to body. There was nowhere to go.

I began to get pushed and shoved violently from all directions as people became more panicked and scared, desperate to escape. I could feel Fred's hands on my back, urging me forward the whole time, guiding me and keeping me on my feet. I realized that we had gotten close to the inner set of swinging doors near the ticket booth, which was just inside the main entrance.

"GO! GO!" Fred screamed behind me. I was hardly aware that a fire alarm had been blaring until I realized that I could hardly hear him. Still, to this day, I can clearly hear Fred yelling this in my ear. These were the last words he spoke to me.

The crush of the bodies was squeezing us apart, and then Fred gave me one last massive shove. Right after this, I felt his hand slip from my back. I immediately turned and looked behind me, but he was gone.

I could no longer see the flames. They were blotted out by the heavy smoke, which continued to drop lower and lower to the ground. It was getting harder and harder to breathe. From this death cloud an alien molten rain fell, dropping down from above like "black rain." I could hear light bulbs explode and large glass windows being broken. I caught brief glimpses of the people closest to me. Their heads were all on fire. It didn't appear that they even realized it. I did not know that my own hair had ignited and was burning at that moment. Like me, they were scared and just wanted to get out of this inferno. The heat was overwhelming and the gas was suffocating, but adrenaline kept everyone pushing forward.

I felt no pain. As odd as that may seem, it just wasn't registering. Whether my body was going into shock or if some kind of survival mechanism had kicked in, I couldn't tell you. I had never been in a situation like that before. Never have I been in fear of my life, facing the reality of my own death. Such thoughts of mortality, always fleeting at best, never seem real. It was creeping closer to me now, and I could not dismiss the reality of my situation.

It was surreal. People were running off in all different directions with their clothes and hair on fire. Some, realizing that their path was blocked, turned and headed in another direction. But there was nowhere to go. We were all trapped. People were calling for help. I was yelling Fred's name, but I could not hear the sound of my own voice over the screaming.

I could only get as far as the ticket counter, but reversing directions against the tide of people to explore other avenues of escape in the darkness and closer to the fire was not an option. The front entrance and cool fresh air was in sight, I just could not get there. All movement had stopped completely. It was a total bottleneck. People were scrambling so frantically to get out through the main doors that some were pushed or fell to the floor in the threshold. In the frenzy, they were trampled and could not get back up. As others tried to scramble over them, they too became wedged in a tangle of bodies that resembled a living, kicking and screaming human wall. The exit quickly became plugged completely, preventing anyone else from escaping and dooming the rest of us still inside.

With forward progress stopped ahead, the pressure from behind was increasing as people tried to force their way out. It became a struggle for me just to stay on my feet. I knew I couldn't resist this force forever, and that once I was on the ground I would have no chance whatsoever. If I wasn't crushed or burned, I was simply going to run out of air. My breathing had become more and more labored as the fire continued to burn out of control, consuming all the oxygen with it. I struggled to get enough air into my lungs. I felt like a fish out of water. I thought, *this is it. This is where I'm going to die.*

It was very strange, and hard to describe now. I hadn't given up, but it I knew I was close to death and I might not make it out. At that moment, my mind just seemed to accept this as inevitable. As if it was preparing me for that fate, all I could think of was Nicholas and Alex. I saw their faces and I prayed to God for them to have a good life and to allow them to forgive me for dying this way and leaving them without their mother. I remember feeling very peaceful, and as this calmness washed over me I fell. I don't know if I was pushed or if I blacked out, but my head struck the floor and that was it. It seemed to happen in slow motion. I remember it clearly, the feeling on falling and the impact of my head on the hardwood. I thought I was dead.

CHAPTER 4   ALTERED STATE

At some point after rescuers arrived at the scene, I was pulled from the burning building by person or persons unknown. It could have been a fire fighter or someone who had escaped and was assisting rescuers pulling people from the inferno. There were many people who risked their safety and their lives in these efforts. Anybody could have saved me, but there is no real way of knowing for sure. There were so many people hurt, it was chaos. And although I was fully conscious in the moments after I was rescued, I have no recollection of any of it.

It was not trauma-induced amnesia that has kept me from recalling the physical and emotional state I was in during this time. As it happened, I was in an altered state from a heavy dose of a powerful sedative drug called Ativan, which I had been administered shortly after I was pulled from the fire and triaged on the scene. This highly-addictive hypnotic medication is very effective in treating anxiety and is widely prescribed to cancer patients to combat nausea and other chemotherapy-related side effects. But the patient's memory also gets wiped out. In my case, it was used to prevent me from feeling any pain so that I could be treated for my severe burn injuries. It was also the beginning stages of a comatose state that my doctors would ease me into with other more powerful drugs.

As I was being transported from the mobile triage center to Miriam Hospital in Providence, another victim who had been in the ambulance with me later told me that I was alert and speaking to the EMT, telling him that I was carrying identification, my license, along with some money and a set of keys in the front pocket of my jeans. The woman told me I kept talking about my sons, and that I insisted someone call them to make sure they were okay.

This ambulance ride to the hospital, like everything else that happened to me after my head struck the floor inside the burning nightclub, I've tried but have been unable to recall.

I also wasn't aware at that time that the heat from the flames had altered my appearance and rendered me all but unrecognizable.

My skin was burnt and swollen, even under my clothes. The wounds were weeping, and any exposed areas of skin not destroyed by heat and fire was black with soot. My own mother would not have known that this person in the ambulance was her daughter.

I was one of the more easily identified survivors only because I had my driver's license on me. This was the only reason that woman in the ambulance knew who I was; she remembered my name from the license after the EMT removed it from my pocket. While everything that happened immediately after the fire has been lost from my memory, I clearly remember taking my ID with me that night. Normally, I never carried any identification. I rarely even carried a purse when I was with Fred because he never let me pay for anything. But for some reason, I stuffed my license along with $20 into my pocket before I left the house.

Once at Miriam Hospital, apparently I was "conscious and combative." This was according to the ER report. My chart also described me as being in a state of *severe agitation*, and because of this they intubated me with a solution that included more Ativan and Morphine.

Because there was a possibility that I could have suffered spine or internal injuries due to trampling, CAT scans of my neck and abdomen were taken as a precaution. These tests revealed no obvious trauma or hemorrhages, so I was transported to the hospital's Intensive Care Unit, where a full catalogue of my burn injuries was taken. At the time, it was estimated that I had burns on 50% of my body. Doctors noted deep second-degree burns to both forearms and hands, as well as full thickness third-degree burns to my left shoulder, the left side of my face and scalp. There was not much remaining of my left ear and my scalp had been burned through to the bone. A bronchoscopy revealed significant smoke inhalation injury with severe secondary burns in all segments of my airways.

To maintain a relative blood pressure, I was intubated with a second IV line in my right femoral artery. I was also placed on a ventilator to help me breath and to combat the symptoms of ARDS (Acute Respiratory Distress Syndrome), which is a life-threatening condition caused by large amounts of fluid collecting in the lungs, a very serious problem that could result in lung failure and death. In the case of a burn victim, the scorching burns and toxic smoke could rupture the small blood vessels in the lungs and allow fluid to leak out of them and into the breathing sacs.

To control the pain, adequate doses of Morphine and Propofol were poured into my body. Other diagnostic tests were taken and treatments prescribed in order to maintain the efficiency of all my body systems.

The swollen, oozing parts of my body that had once been covered with skin were treated with povidone iodine, an antiseptic agent used topically to destroy invading microbes.

All these measures were taken to stabilize my condition and, if I managed to survive all the immediate dangers my body faced, to prepare me for the challenges of healing that lay ahead.

Dr. David Barrall received an early wakeup call at home from Miriam Hospital at 3 a.m. He was initially requested to report to the O.R. to attend to my injuries, but there would be other surgeries for him to perform on fire survivors that morning. He performed the only surgical procedure on me during my short stay at Miriam Hospital, the debridement of the burnt skin on my face and both hands. The physical removal of dead, burned skin is about as painful an experience as a patient can go through. Thankfully, this was also part of a medicated haze that prevented me from remembering or feeling anything whatsoever.

Post-operatively, my face was slathered with an antibiotic ointment and Silvadene cream was applied to my hands. Sterile fluff dressings were placed between my fingers and my hands and arms were loosely wrapped with sterile Kling bandages. I was immediately ushered into the hospital's Intensive Care Unit and attended to by the ICU physicians and staff.

Looking back on all this now, part of me was glad that I was not aware of what was happening to my body that soon after the fire, but the one aspect of the ordeal that I wish I had knowledge about above all else is who pulled me out of the burning building. In the moments before my head struck the hardwood floor I was fully expecting to die. I could not envision being physically saved from a fate that took Fred from me and claimed the lives of so many others, but I'm extremely grateful to whoever had risked their own life to save mine. I wish I was able to properly thank that individual, or individuals, for their bravery and heroism. In my thoughts, I thank that unknown hero every day, and I will continue to do so for the rest of my life. Up to this day, whenever I meet a local fire fighter who was working on February 20, 2003, I thank him or her because it just may have been them who saved me that night.

Putting emotions aside for a moment, and thinking about my rescue rationally, I still don't know how anyone was able to get me out of there at all. I was on the floor. I was close to the pile of bodies at the front door. There had to be other people on top of me, maybe inadvertently protecting me from the full wrath of the flames. Yet I somehow got pulled out alive, when so many others did not. This is why, regardless of the degree of devastation that the fire has had on me personally, I am thankful for a second chance at life. I have so much to live for, so many people who love me and so much I want to accomplish and see my boys accomplish, that I am just happy to have these opportunities available.

This was certainly not always the case, however. When I initially became aware of my condition and situation, I did not possess the same will to live that I do now. In fact, there were many, many times I would have preferred to have died with Fred that night.

Getting back to the early hours after being rescued from the fire, in the state I was in at that time, I didn't have a worry in the world. For my family, however, it was a different story entirely.

My mother had seen some of the earlier news accounts of the fire, and instantly had a bad feeling about it involving her family. However, it was my brother who she became concerned about. She knew he was the one who would have been most likely to have gone to a club like The Station, but she also knew that he was already home safe and sound when the report was being aired. She has had strong premonitions before, so she could not entirely discount this one. Even after she went to bed, she couldn't shake the feeling that something was wrong.

It was just before 2 a.m. when the phone rang at my mom's house. She and my step dad were abruptly awakened and informed by Cranston police that I was in Miriam Hospital with burns I had sustained in The Station fire. They rushed immediately to the hospital, and got in to see me while I was still being evaluated. I was only partially covered, lying on a gurney and sedated. She thought I was dead. My face was charred and black. She never felt more heartache and anguish in her life, just an oppressive sick feeling inside. It was worry to the nth degree.

As she and Vincent were ushered into a small room down the hall to wait for the doctor, she recalled the last time she sat in a room like that at a hospital, the day my dad died.

When the doctor came in he told them that I would probably be transferred a hospital in Boston later that morning and that it would be best if they went home and got some rest. There was nothing they could do there, and the hospital would notify them as soon as a decision was made on my transfer.

There was a phone in the room, and my mom wanted to call some of her family to let them know what happened. But it was still very early. One person she did not want to notify was my ex-husband. She was unsure how he might react. She just didn't want to have Alex and Nicholas go through any more trauma than necessary. She did call Stephanie, who realized there was something wrong when she picked up the phone at four in the morning and heard her mother's voice.

My mom only told her that she and Vincent were on their way over to her house. She wouldn't say anything more, but my sister knew at once that I had been in the fire and she started screaming.

About an hour and a half earlier, Matt woke up to the sound of the television. He and Stephanie had fallen asleep with it on when they went to bed. My brother-in-law was reaching to shut it off when he saw that there was a late-breaking news story on the local station and he paused to see what had happened. A fire at a local rock club prompted him to wake up my sister and ask her if I had gone to The Station after dinner to see Great White. He knew that Fred liked live music. Stephanie told her husband that we had gone to a movie. Besides, she had never heard of Great White and didn't think that I liked them. She was so sure I wasn't there that she didn't think twice about it. She convinced Matt, as well, and the two of them sat up for another hour, mesmerized and horrified by the catastrophe at the nightclub. Very little information was available. They were reporting only three deaths at that time. It was late, so they turned off the television and went back to bed. Forty-five minutes later the phone rang and the screaming started.

There was a lot of emotion and confusion, as you can imagine, and while I had been rescued and identified, Fred's whereabouts were unknown. My family knew I had been with Fred, but they didn't know how to get in contact with anyone from his family.

It was close to 6 a.m. when my bother-in-law and my step dad decided to drive to West Warwick to see if they could learn something about Fred. With the streets blocked off, they parked and walked to scene. Matt figured that if Fred had been one of the fire's three reported victims, it would be obvious. Fred was big guy, 6'2" and over 250 pounds. As they got nearer, Matt approached a state trooper and began to explain why they were there. After he told the trooper that I had been found and that Fred was still missing, he began to describe Fred. The trooper gave him an incredulous look and stopped him at once. "Sir," he said. "There are over 70 people dead in there."

The news floored them. They had no idea of the scope of the tragedy that was continuing to unfold. Few did at that time. The high number of deaths was just starting to circulate in the news. Matt and Vinny also learned that the police were still trying to determine who may have been at the club that night by cross referencing the license plates of the cars in the parking lots with the owners of the vehicles. Matt was asked if Fred or I had driven that night, but he didn't know. He ended up driving to Fred's house in Warwick, where he spotted Fred's new truck in the driveway, so they knew I had taken my car.

It was also around 6 a.m. when my mother received word from Miriam that I was going to be transported to Shriners Burns Hospital in Boston. There are twenty-two Shriners Hospitals throughout the U. S., providing specialized pediatric care in one of these areas: spinal cord injury rehabilitation; cleft lip and palate treatment; orthopedic care; burn care. All the facilities are 100% privately funded and they are simply the best at what they do. For only the second time in the 80-year history of Shriners Burns Hospitals they were opening their doors to adult burn victims. The first time was after the terrorist attacks on 9-11, when Shriners in New York was ready to receive the injured, but of course there were no survivors of any age to admit that day. Now, in the wake of The Station Nightclub Fire, they admitted four adult survivors, including myself. I needed more specialized care than Miriam Hospital could provide, and I would have otherwise gone directly to Massachusetts General but all of their beds were full, many with Station Fire survivors.

I was in critical condition when I was discharged from Miriam, but I was carefully prepped to make the fifty mile trip to Boston. A few short hours after I had arrived, I left the hospital in a much different state of being. I was neither combative nor agitated, thanks to a 10 mg. per hour Morphine drip and a 500 cc Propofol chaser for added comfort. I was transported by ambulance and arrived at Shriners by nine o'clock. I was on mechanical life support and went straight to their intensive care unit.

Meanwhile, my family had managed to contact Fred's sister, Nancy, from an address book that I kept at the house. When Matt discovered Fred's house key on my key chain, he made arrangements to meet Fred's family at his house later that morning to let them inside.

As Matt approached Fred's house, he saw a Warwick police cruiser pulling out of Fred's driveway. The police stopped the car and asked where he was going. Matt explained to the officer the situation with Fred's family and the key.

Matt knew something was wrong by the expression on the face of the young officer, who said that he was on his way to contact the landlord at the request of a family member who needed a key to gain access into the house. My brother-in-law thought that was odd, and didn't put it together right away, but as it turned out someone was trying to rob Fred and using the police to do it. The robber was supposed to meet the police back at the house later that day, after the key had been secured. The would-be robber, however, never returned, so to this day we don't know who had tried such a risky and stupid ploy. One thing is certain, the person knew Fred well enough to appreciate the value of his sports collection, and must also have known that Fred had gone to The Station the night before, figuring that he at least had been injured in the fire and that this was a perfect opportunity for looting. It's hard to imagine how anyone could do something like that to a person who might have gotten hurt or killed in a horrible tragedy.

A little later that morning, my family gathered and drove together to visit me at the hospital. They all piled into a minivan and made the hour long trip to Boston.

When they were finally able to get a glimpse of me, they could not have expected what they saw. I was wrapped like a mummy and my body had swollen to three times its normal size, which made them question if it was even me that they were looking at. It could have been anybody under those heavy bandages.

It was a sad fact that early on many of The Station fire survivors were being misidentified, including Fred, whose sister Nancy was originally told by the hospital where he had been taken that he was alive. However, she would learn that this was a mistake, and that the survivor they thought was Fred was not him. It turned out to be a woman, in fact. There was so much confusion, and it added a terrible strain to an already unfathomable situation. Initially, after having been given hope that her brother had survived the tragedy, the news that the fire had claimed Fred's life was even more devastating.

In order to avoid this problem with me, my mother and my sister identified me by the tattoo they knew I had on my right ankle. Although they couldn't agree whether I had a rose or a heart tattoo, when the nurse unwrapped the lower part of my right leg, they all agreed it was me.

My family was later given the clothes I had been wearing and was surprised to see that they were largely intact, and not burnt through. Considering the condition I was in, it did not seem possible that my jeans and top would look so good.

While I may not have been suffering at that particular moment, the people closest to me were living a cruel nightmare, not knowing if I was going to remain a survivor of The Station Fire or become another victim.

Shriners, however, did everything that they could for their visitors as well as their patients. They made an impossible situation tolerable for my family. It was difficult for them to appreciate everything that the facility did for them while they were there because they were in shock for much of the time. When there was time to reflect, however, they were roundly amazed by the treatment they received. From the moment they walked through the double doors of the main entrance they were never alone. They were immediately assigned a counselor who saw to it that every question they had was answered, every concern they expressed was addressed. Whatever they may have needed, the people at Shriners found a way to meet that need. The only thing my family really wanted was to have me walk out through their double doors on my own as quickly as possible. This happened to be the exact same goal that everyone at Shriners was working toward, as well.

They understood what it was like for someone to watch a loved one go through the trauma of burn survival. After all, they have helped untold numbers of people recover from every kind of burn possible for nearly a century, and when I was wheeled in through Shriners' emergency entrance only hours before my family arrived, they didn't know what to expect.

My family got through this with me, but first my family had to get through it themselves. It was Shriners who helped them, getting them through hour by hour, then day by day. All the while, the doctors and staff never pulled any punches. They didn't just tell my family what they wanted to hear. There were some hard truths, but my family found that they could cope with all of it, in part because they trusted that the hospital was doing everything it could for me.

Because the facility treats young burn victims from all over the world, one thing the hospital does to makes things a little easier, and a lot more convenient, for parents is to provide them with apartment units located on the premises. They gave my mother and step dad an apartment, but over the course of my stay at Shriners, it was shared by other family members, especially Stephanie and Matt, who stayed there in rotating shifts around work and family obligations.

Matt and Stephanie have four children, Matt, Brianna, Dylan and Ryan, who would often come up on the weekends when my boys visited. Alex and Nicholas didn't see me at this stage, it would have been too traumatic for them, but there were near. There was, however, a playroom at the hospital where the children congregated, children of Station Fire survivors and other Shriners' patients, some were burn victims themselves, but they all played together. It was remarkable to see them having so much fun in a setting like that.

There were other inherent advantages to being at a children's hospital, as my family found out. There was one time, after they had just received some not so good news about my condition after I had developed a dangerous infection, when they stepped off the elevator into the lobby and saw a clown sitting in a wing chair. An actual clown with a big grin, red nose, clown makeup, clown shoes, everything. They couldn't help but smile when they saw that, especially with children all around laughing and giggling.

For me, it was touch and go early on, even though I could not have been in a better place. Shriners was well-equipped to not only treat the injuries I had suffered but to save my life, which was a real concern and their only priority when I first arrived. My condition was very serious, and there was a good chance that I would not make it. My survival depended on how my body responded to the trauma in the first twenty-four hours. And it did not look good. My doctors were wary, but every patient is different, and there was no way to know which way my condition would go. Every hour that passed decreased the odds against me exponentially. So it became a waiting game to see if I would live or die. There was a lot that could go wrong. Damage to major internal organs and subsequent death was a constant threat.

Severe, large burns wreak havoc on every system of the body, particularly respiration and circulation. For doctors, it's a delicate balancing act keeping a burn victim alive. These breaches of our body's protective barrier not only provide germs with an easy access inside, but it permits vital fluids to continually escape, which results in massive swelling.

This inflammation is part of the body's attempt to heal itself, but it can cause problems of its own by collapsing veins in the extremities. When that happens, blood backs up and arteries no longer function, setting up clotting conditions that can kill.

The same burns that trigger this calamity also causes pores to open in the vessels and proteins to leak out, taking more fluid with them. A patient needs to have this life-giving fluid replaced, even as it is leaking out and causing swelling. The more fluid that is put back into the body, the more swelling occurs, and the greater the risk of clotting. It's a vicious cycle that can confuse the body, which sometimes doesn't know what to do to save itself. It's a tricky proposition for a physician, as well.

The fluid leaking out of the vessels also causes a significant drop in blood pressure, and if not enough blood and oxygen reach the kidneys, renal failure can occur.

Large burns will increase the body's metabolism two to three times its normal rate by trying to keep itself warm. A body with badly damaged skin is like a house with no roof; heat escapes freely. That's why operating rooms at the burn centers are routinely kept at temperatures of 80 to 100 degrees. Similar to turning up the thermostat in the roofless house to keep it warm, the body tries to regulate an optimal functioning temperature of around 98.6 degrees by burning massive stores of energy. Once the body has used up the easily available energy, it begins to feed on itself, including its lean muscle mass, a process called catabolism.

When this occurs, and the body switches over to using its own proteins to supply energy, the hospital staff must combat the body's defenses by supplying the burn victim with more protein and more nutritional supplements and vitamins. It often becomes a struggle for the bodies of some patients to get enough of these fluids to maintain proper organ and system function. As a further complication, excessive proteins can be harmful to the kidneys, so that has to be carefully monitored.

Initially, in order to preserve my body heat, I was intubated and wrapped up like a mummy in thick swatches of antimicrobial bandages which acted as my temporary skin. Before more permanent skin could be considered, removing the dead skin and keeping the bandages fresh and clean were important for any hope of survival I had.

From the moment I was pulled from the fire that Friday night, I was in grave danger of not surviving the injuries I had sustained, and the doctors and nurses were faced with the challenge of sustaining my life by keeping my body from turning on itself and shutting down. To help facilitate that entire healing process, I was being given increasing doses of barbiturates that would ease me into a coma from which I would not emerge from for nearly three months.

The following day, Saturday, my condition did not improve. By Sunday, I had taken a turn for the worse. All my organs began shutting down, and short of organ replacement there was nothing that could be done about it. Doctors advised my entire family to come to the hospital because I was not going to make it through the night. I was read my last rites.

I was barely conscious and all but unaware that I was on death's door, but I can't begin to describe what my family, my mother, sister and children, were going through when they were informed that I was going to die and they needed to prepare for this eventuality. My brother-in-law was given the task by the social worker to break the news to my children. I still have a card that Alex and Nicholas would have been given if I had died. It was an attempt to explain to a child in simple but unqualified language the meaning of death. The message read like a Dr. Seuss meets Dr. Kevorkian approach to child psychology, and basically told them that it was time for Mommy to go away. I don't like thinking about the pain and trauma my children went through during that time. It just breaks my heart.

My oldest, Alex, after hearing that his mother was going to die, asked one of his aunts to bring him to the chapel at Shriners. He went in alone and had a conversation with God. To this day, he hasn't told me what he said, but when he walked out of the chapel he was smiling. He told his aunt with confidence that his mom was going to be fine, that I was going to live.

CHAPTER 5   A WORLD OF MY OWN

Two nights after the fire, Jeffrey Derderian, The Station co-owner, gave a sobbing press conference, expressing his sympathy and heartache over the tragic fire. He made a terse denial of having knowledge or granting permission for the use of pyrotechnics by the band. This would be the first of many contradictory statements and reports regarding this matter in the following weeks, months and years. Lead singer, Jack Russell, claimed that he had gotten permission for the fireworks display, which the band uses at almost all of their shows. While several other club owners at venues where Great White had recently played denied having been asked permission by the band, some claiming complete surprise, other musical acts openly admitted that they had used fireworks at The Station numerous times in the past. A local firefighter even came forward to say that he had been stationed at the West Warwick club as many as seven times over the past year for that very reason.

The response from officials around the state was swift. Anyone not in a coma could hear the proverbial barn door swinging shut after the horses had escaped. Those ranking highest and with the most to lose made the most noise. Patrick Lynch, the Rhode Island Attorney General and Governor Donald Carcieri immediately began sounding off, promising to bring criminal charges against all those responsible. The grand jury convened even before the embers cooled at the site of the fire. As blame was being spread far and wide, possible defendants scurried like cockroaches for protection and attorneys across the region were summoned. The club owners, the band members, the foam and pyrotechnics manufacturers and distributors, state and city officials and others were all fair game.

On February 26, Californian Jack Russell was back in Rhode Island for the first time since the fire. He and other band members, as well as tour manager Daniel Biechele, were there at the behest of the grand jury that was looking into criminal actions associated with The Station fire. These individuals were high on the list of people whose actions were directly responsible for the fire. It was not an accident. It wasn't something that just happened. It should never have happened. If these people had acted differently, acted properly, then one hundred people would have survived the night of February 20, 2003. The band knew about pyrotechnics, and it stands to reason that they knew how dangerous they were. Jack Russell wasn't just the band's lead singer, he was its founder and someone who was responsible for making the decision to light dangerous fireworks inside a crowded building. He should have thought twice and scrapped the pyrotechnics for that one night.

Though Russell was present at the National Guard complex in East Greenwich, R. I., where the grand jury was meeting, the lead singer did not testify that day. His lawyer, Neil Philbin, met with state prosecutors to find out what questions his client would be asked and to inquire about a possible immunity deal, which would guarantee that Russell would not be criminally charged in exchange for his testimony. Such deals are not uncommon. After all, Russell could be subpoenaed to appear before the grand jury only to invoke his Fifth Amendment right against self-incrimination and give them nothing. This was likely what Russell would have done, as he was a certain target of the criminal and civil proceedings to follow. An immunity deal, at the very least, would ensure that he spoke publicly about what he had known and didn't know. Immunity deals are generally considered a win-win for both sides, but in this case it would have been devastating if Russell and his band were not held accountable to some degree and were not subject to the consequences of their wrongdoing.

The day after members of Great White returned to Rhode Island with their lawyers, exactly a week after the fire, a prayer vigil was organized for me by my co-workers in the Department of Pediatrics. Other Rhode Island Hospital employees attended the healing service, as well. I had no way of knowing that so many people were thinking of me, praying for me and donating their time, money and various gifts to my family.

Everywhere, people were so helpful and thoughtful, giving my family that much less to worry about. My mother's phone rang nonstop for days as friends and family from all over offered their well-wishes. She even got a call from her cousins in Italy who saw news footage of the fire and recognized The Station. During a previous trip to visit their American cousins they had gone to the nightclub (under different ownership then) with me, my sister and my brother.

My neighbors Meryl Sears and Carole Manzi organized a neighborhood donation drive, assisted by my friend, Doreen Aceto. They collected money, food, gift certificates and gas cards from around the community, which responded generously to their requests. The many letters of support and faith could have been stacked up twenty feet high.

Teachers in the Oaklawn school system made an extra effort to be sure that my two sons were looked after and did not miss out on their schooling. They even visited the boys at home and brought them donated toys. The PTA presented gift baskets and food. People cooked, baby sat and did everything that I could not do for Alex and Nicholas at that time.

While all this was going on, some people at the hospital were waiting for me to die. My family had been told to prepare for the worst, but they were hoping for a miracle. Part of the preparation included doing a lot of things that nobody enjoys. Paperwork had to be filed for health insurance, life insurance in case I did die, as well as social security benefits. My two boys had to be considered first and foremost, so lawyers had to be contacted so that their best interests could be represented.

My brother-in-law stepped forward to see to it that these matters were taken care of. As a Type A personality, Matt fell into this role naturally enough. Fortunately, I was very organized and he was able to find all the information he needed in one drawer of my filing cabinet. The state also made things as easy as possible for family members who were trying to do exactly what my brother-in-law was attempting. They provided instant access to available funds as well as resources so that filings could be done efficiently and swiftly, and all of this in a one-stop location.

When things looked the bleakest, my doctors decided to try a new type of ventilator on me. It had never been used on someone in my condition, but they figured there was nothing to lose. They had no way of knowing what was going to happen, though they obviously thought there was some possibility that the ventilator might be able to help me. This last ditch effort to save my life proved to be the miracle my family had been praying for.

When new, more flexible fiber optic scopes were threaded down into my lungs, they revealed in great detail the severity of my inhalation injuries. What was causing me the biggest problem was that my lungs were coated with a thick tarry substance which was hindering my ability to breath. What this ventilator did was use a special solution of nitric acid to help break up this substance. With the tar gone, my blood vessels could dilate and deliver more oxygen to my starving organs.

Within just a couple of hours, my vital organs, including my liver and kidney began to show some signs of improvement, enough anyway for doctors to tell my family that there was some hope. It *was* miraculous. Truly unexpected, anyway. The doctors told my family that there was some hope.

I continued to improve slowly. Within about a week, my vital organs were able to function sufficiently on their own. I remained on a ventilator, however, because my lungs were far from clear and I could not breathe on my own.

Under the care of the entire Shriners' staff, in particular the Assistant Chief of Staff, Dr. Robert Sheridan, as well as Dr. John Schulz and Dr. Colleen Ryan, I couldn't have been in more capable hands. There were many other physicians, nurses, staff members and caregivers who were involved in my treatment and recovery and I was lucky to have them when I needed them. Every one of these people, as far as I'm concerned, are among the most incredibly gifted and caring people in the world. What they did for me, and what they have no doubt done for many other people before and since me, was not just their jobs. It goes far beyond that. And I owe them my life. I owe them everything.

I was the first fire survivor to have received treatment from this ventilator, and as a result it is now used regularly to save lives. It is something I'm proud to be a part of, especially when I hear from doctors who use it and patients that are alive today because of it.

It was at this point that I was intentionally eased into a medically-induced coma. Although I didn't have far to go, this was done in order to make the recovery process less traumatic for my body and allow me to heal without suffering any pain.

Outside the hospital, the world continued to turn. It did not stop for me. Bills had to be paid. Fortunately, because of my loving family and my health insurance from work, my son's basic needs could be met. Although, just as I remained wholly unaware of this crisis in my own home, I was equally oblivious to the scope of suffering that was going on around the state. As funerals, prayer vigils and memorials were being held all around the state for the fire victims, Governor Carcieri reached out to the federal government for disaster relief money to help the many families who were in need of assistance during this time. The Governor had petitioned the Federal Emergency Management Agency (FEMA) immediately after the fire, and that request was summarily rejected. It was the government's opinion that The Station Fire was not a "major disaster," at least as defined under the Robert T. Stafford Disaster Relief Act, which *requires a major disaster declaration to be based on a disaster of such severity and magnitude that effective response is beyond (a local government's or state's) capabilities.*

According to this criterion, The Station Nightclub Fire did not apply. Besides, FEMA director Joe Albaugh told Governor Carcieri that the federal government had already provided assistance to Rhode Island when the Department of Health and Human Services provided two dozen pathologists to help identify victims of the fire.

I guess that was enough for a Democratic state during a Republican presidency.

To that end, it should be noted that the President of the United States has the authority to declare federal disasters under the Robert T. Stafford Disaster Relief Act.

A month after the fire, another appeal was made to President Bush requesting financial aid. The governor felt he was more prepared this time, including all the necessary information and facts with his petition, something that he realized had been lacking in the previous application. This was the reason he believed they turned him down so quickly in February. His second request was also rejected, though not as quickly.

Around this time, something else happened that could not have been entirely unexpected. During more recent times of any social disaster or individual misfortune, if there is anything you can count on it's the presence of lawyers. Many people don't like them, until they need them, and with so many people who were affected by this fire there was no way to avoid the march of the lawsuits that would follow. It didn't take long. In early March 2003, the first lawsuits were filed by lawyers on behalf of victims' families and survivors.

A criminal investigation was also underway and the grand jury probe continued, subpoenaing witnesses and gathering information. Fire and safety inspectors were running around the state like chickens with their heads off, writing citations and closing down public facilities for violating various infractions. Lawmakers dropped everything to try to bolster building and safety regulations, such as repealing all "grandfather" laws on older facilities. No building should be forgiven for lagging behind the public safety codes, not anymore, not after The Station fire.

As part of the ongoing criminal investigation, evidence was carefully sifted through before being removed from the site of the fire and taken to a 4,000 square-foot warehouse in Cranston about 8 miles away. Hundreds of pieces of evidence were catalogued and stored, with some portions of the club's interior reconstructed with original material. The lawyers petitioned for access to this evidence for use in the preparation of the lawsuits.

A group of lawyers from the firm of Mandell, Schwartz & Boisclair were preparing to handle my personal litigation. They would be representing me in all civil actions and handling any money awarded to me for damages and other compensation. What I later found completely astounding was that Liberty Mutual, my health/life insurer, sent a Notice of Lien to my lawyers officially asserting their right to be reimbursed for any payments which they might make to me out of any recovery moneys that I might receive as a result of my injuries.

So here I was, in a coma and barely alive, and my insurance company was preparing a strategy to be reimbursed for money they might be responsible for paying my family as a result of my injuries, or in the event of my death. The line was forming already for money that would come from this catastrophe of lost life and ruined bodies. Thankfully, they have since decided to remove this lien.

Meanwhile, my physical existence continued in a strange limbo between life and death. Debriding was a ritual that continued while I was heavily sedated and in a coma, a process that is much easier on everyone in this state. The skin is a complex and fascinating organ, the largest organ of the human body and one that is perhaps most often taken for granted. It does so much for us, and it is only when it is damaged that we realize just how important it is to our survival. I was glad, however, that I was not conscious while undergoing the process of debridement during this time.

Most of my burns penetrated the dermis, the second of the two main layers of cells that make up the skin. This layer is filled with tiny nerves that sense touch, temperature, pressure and pain. The dermis is also filled with tiny blood vessels, hair follicles, sweat glands which help regulate body temperature, and oil glands that secrete a substance which helps keep our skin from drying out. When the dermis is damaged these tiny nerves and blood vessels are exposed, making burns very sensitive to pain and temperature changes and allows fluid to leak from the capillaries.

Dead skin is also a haven for bacteria to grow, and that's why this skin needs to be removed frequently. It's ironic that burn patients are always cold, so debridement is performed in rooms that are very warm. The important dual role of our skin is demonstrated when it can no longer effectively perform these two functions, keeping heat in and germs out.

There are several methods of debridement, but for me it involved a nurse carefully unwrapping my bandages and bathing the burn areas with warm antiseptic water to rinse off the dead skin. A painstaking, but effective procedure, my debridement took several hours to complete, after which the areas are heavily bandaged once again with sterile dressings. This treatment is repeated twice a day or more, until the skin starts to heal on its own. If this doesn't happen, then skin grafting is necessary. Skin grafts effectively replace burned skin with new skin.

Doctors performed ten skin grafts while I was comatose.

These operations may not be the most glamorous, but skin grafting is a very important part of burns healing. Without it, a burn could take many painful months to heal with an increased risk of infection and death.

The surgeons who perform these procedures deserve much more adoration than they receive. What they do is not easy. It's tedious, gruesome and physically demanding.

Having to reposition a patient during the course of any surgery is difficult and dangerous, but is seldom necessary. In burn surgery, however, it's done all the time. A burn can be on one side of the body and the donor site on the other, and each time a patient is moved a changing of all sterile drapes is required. Everyone inside the operating room must also change their gowns and gloves. Time-consuming, but essential.

The work is bloody and the surgeons must wear impervious sterile garments in an operating room where temperatures are set around 90-degrees.

In years past, skin grafting was not routinely performed on a burn victim. It was common practice to allow the patient's body to heal itself, let it slough off the burned flesh and regrow new skin. While this is the ideal way for skin to heal, the problem is infection. Because it takes time for the body to regrow skin, the longer it takes the more opportunity infections have to invade the injury sites. Amputations and death often result from letting this process play itself out for too long. Today, things are done differently. More superficial burn wounds will heal on their own, but deep second and full thickness burns require skin graft surgery for quick healing and minimal scarring.

A patient's ability to withstand this type of surgery is major factor that burn surgeons consider before undergoing the procedure. Sustaining life always takes precedence.

Once the decision for skin grafting is made, it is time to harvest new skin. Harvesting skin from a donor site is as gruesome and as painful as you can imagine.

Grafting begins by removing healthy skin from a patient's body, called a donor site, using an instrument called a dermatome, similar to an electric shaver. This oscillating blade gently shaves off thin layers of skin, about 10-15/1000 of an inch. A lot smaller than deli-sliced cold cuts. If the patient needs to be turned to access the burn area to which the harvested skin is going to be grafted, that is done at this time. The dead skin is then removed from the area, after which it is cleaned and prepared for grafting.

There are actually two types of skin grafts, *sheet* and *meshed*. Because skin is elastic, the removed piece will shrink nearly in half. The donor skin is sometimes put through a mesher, a special machine that has two rollers, similar to those old metal mop buckets. This type is called a *meshed graft*. This mesher machine cuts tiny "X" patterns into the skin, like page perforations, so it can be stretched, up to nine times its original size.

The stretched donor skin is then placed over the burn site and is held in place with skin staples or Steri-Strips. Over time, the patient's own cells will eventually fill in the spaces that were cut by the mesher, but the crisscross patterns never completely fade.

You can get as much use as possible out of a small section of skin with meshed grafting. However, when grafting is done to the face and neck, areas that are most often exposed, this "meshing" step is skipped and the donor site skin is grafted to the area as it is, one unstretched piece at a time. This is called *sheet grafting*. This was what had been done to me. My grafts were held in place with staples.

If healthy skin is plentiful and grafting needs to be done in 20% or less of the entire patient's body area, the meshing step is often skipped, as well. But when burn areas are extensive and available donor sites are minimal, meshing is done to maximize coverage. Meshed grafted skin is not as pliable or cosmetically appealing as sheet grafting.

With meshed grafts, thin web-like mesh gauze, called bridal veil, is placed over the graft site to protect the exposed skin layer. This material will dry onto the wound to act as a scab until the donor site is healed, just as real skin would. Sheet grafts are not covered with bridal veil.

In choosing donor sites for harvesting, the least visible areas of the body, if any, are always chosen first, such as the thicker skin on the sole of a patient's feet. Mine were taken from the front and back of my upper legs.

Meshed grafts and sheet grafts are both forms of autograft, which is skin taken from the burn patient, and used to cover wounds permanently. Since the skin is a major organ in the body, an autograft is essentially an organ transplant.

There are a variety of other graft techniques to consider.

Skin donated by other people who have died is called homograft, allograft, or cadaver skin, and it is sometimes used as a temporary cover for a burn or wound before permanent autograft placement.

Xenograft or Heterograft is skin taken from a variety of animals, usually a pig. Heterograft skin became popular because of the limited availability and high expense of human skin tissue. In some cases religious, financial, or cultural objections to the use of human cadaver skin may also be factors. Wound coverage using xenograft or heterograft is also a temporary covering until autograft is performed.

With both meshed or sheet grafts, burn surgeons are careful of the size and placement of the harvested skin, as well as the stapled edges, not only to limit scarring but for range of motion considerations, as scars can interfere with range of motion.

Burns are often more comfortable after being covered with a skin graft, but burn patients feel more pain from donor sites than from grafted areas. It stings and itches terribly, like the worst rug rash burn you can imagine.

Afterward, if you're conscious, you are given pain medicine to keep you as comfortable as possible. Your new skin grafts are very fragile. You may lose blood during or soon after the surgery from the tiny capillaries in your skin. Often burn patients need blood transfusions to replace blood lost during surgery. Blood transfusions increase the number of red blood cells, which carry oxygen from the lungs to every part of the body and take waste in the form of carbon dioxide back to the lungs, where it is breathed out into the air. If there aren't enough red blood cells or if the cells do not contain enough iron to carry oxygen properly, wounds do not heal as well.

To further help the graft heal and become secure, the area of the graft, and essentially the patient, is not moved for five days following each surgery. During this immobilization period, blood vessels begin to grow from the tissue below into the donor skin, bonding the two layers together. Five days after grafting, exercise therapy programs, tub baths and other normal daily activities resume. Donor sites take about ten days to heal and the skin to grow back. The same area can then be harvested again, once again limiting donor site scarring.

Beside the debridements and skin graft surgeries, I had numerous operations on my hands and arms to help preserve and improve the circulation in order to avert amputation. Scar revision and reconstructive surgery usually followed some of my heavier skin grafting operations.

As I slept, I was treated for the damage done to my lungs as well as my skin. Some of the worst burns, and hardest to treat, were in the throats of survivors. These kinds of inhalation injuries scorch the windpipe so badly that it can swell shut or fill the lungs with enough soot to choke off breathing. With every artificial respiration, a continuous flow of a viscous black substance flowed out of my lungs and into a bag at the side of my bed.

As I was going through all this at Shriners, I was truly in a world all my own, but I was never alone. My family was always there. There was always someone in my room, talking to me, whether it was words of encouragement or just chit chat, telling me what was going in the world or some neighborhood gossip. My room had to be the loudest in the hospital, even if all the conversations were one-sided.

My family never gave up on me. Even after more than a month with the best medical care any burn patient could possibly ask for, there was still no guarantee that I was going to survive. One day I could be showing signs of improvement and the next everything could change completely. My family could never relax. The most minor setback could start me on a downward spiral from which I might never recover.

In early March, soon after a skin graft was performed on my shoulder, I developed a fever that spiked to 105-degrees. But my temperature was quickly brought under control and normalized. During the second week of March, another complication arose when I developed pneumonia. My body was able to win this fight as well during the course of the next week. But how much longer could my luck hold out?

The uncertainty of what each day might bring was becoming increasingly wearisome, and the emotional responses varied widely from family member to family member. My mom was beside herself with grief. My sister could not stop crying. My youngest son was in denial that his mom was going to be taken away from him permanently. My brother-in-law became angry.

Worse still, they could only wonder what my life would be like if I did survive. They could not even tell what I looked like under all those bandages. Only the tips of my blackened fingers and nose were exposed. How my own emotional and psychological state would cope with the horrible disfiguring and debilitating burns I suffered they could only guess. Would I have to be on machines for the rest of my life? Would I be able to eat on my own? Would I be able to take care of myself or be dependent on others, and have to be placed in a nursing facility?

These quality of life concerns were real. For all that the hospital provided, my family members had seen children with burns so horrible that they barely resembled anything human. It sounds harsh, but to see these kinds of burns, it's difficult to imagine a person living anything close to a normal life. Some of them had no faces to speak of, or were missing one or more limbs. These were sad, humbling sites for my family to witness.

They met a fourteen-month old boy who had been left on the doorstep of an orphanage in China. He had been badly burned and had been wrapped in a burial cloth when he was found. The child was adopted by the owner's of the orphanage and flown from this desolate village in China by Shriners for treatment. The child didn't have health insurance. Neither the orphanage nor the people who ran it had the kind of resources it took to make something like that happen. This was what Shriners does. This is what they are all about. And there are stories after stories like this, children from all over the world who are taken in by Shriners and cared for by the best of the best.

With all the hours my family spent at Shriners, they got to meet many of the other survivors and their families and became close with some of them, including the parents of Joe DiBona. The fire, given all its death and destruction, brought together these people who would develop such a strong bond that they would remain the very best of friends to this day. It amazes me every time I think about it, with everything that was going on around Joe and me while we were asleep our families were forming this friendship. How something so tragic could also bring something so positive and lasting is beyond my comprehension, but I know that I will always be grateful for all of the love and support our families gave us and each other.

CHAPTER 6   BUBBLE GIRL

On March 24, I was given a temporary tracheostomy and a tube was inserted directly into my windpipe to assist my damaged lungs. Soon afterward, while still comatose, I was prepared for a move to another hospital, Massachusetts General, where beds were becoming available. I was not out of the woods by any means, but there was no danger to me being moved.

My stay as well as my family's stay at Shriners was over, and although I remember none of it, it was a life-changing experience. My time there also left a lasting impression on others.

Alyson Musco is now a RN at Shriners Burns Hospital for Children in Boston, but in March 2003 she was a Northeastern University nursing student. She always felt a calling to be a nurse and to help people, and at Shriners she figured she could do the most good working in the Acute Care Unit, dealing with children who were still in their initial burn treatment time frame. When she finally got on the unit, things were slow for the first month or so. Then, on the night February 20, 2003 she had gone to bed early and did not catch any of that night's newscasts about the fire. She was awakened around 5 a.m. the following morning by a phone call from the hospital and informed that they were waiving the age limit and admitted victims of the Rhode Island nightclub fire. She was asked if she could come in and she did immediately.

The day that I left Shriners, Alyson was working with my nurse, assisting in my care in preparation for my transfer. After they had finished with my dressings, the nurse told Alyson, "I am going to teach you one of the most important parts of our job. It doesn't have to do with meds, or dressings, or tube feedings. It has to do with treating a comatose patient, on a ventilator, like a human being, and in this case, like a woman, like someone's daughter, like someone's mother."

At that moment Alyson recalled sitting at the nurse's desk one afternoon, directly across from my room, where my two sons were standing outside the sliding glass doors that separated them from me. She could not help overhearing Alex and Nicholas talking to me as if they were right beside me. Since Shriners is a pediatric facility, it was quite a shock to see children visiting their parents. For Alyson, listening to a little boy tell his mother how much he loves her was beyond heartbreaking and beyond heartwarming at the same time.

"People don't stop being people because they are unconscious or can't communicate back," the nurse lectured Alyson. "Don't ever forget that."

And with that, the nurse took out a bar of soap and two razors. "I'll start with the right leg, you do the left," she said. For the next hour they pampered me like I was at a spa. They lathered me up and shaved my legs.

This is exactly what I would want someone to do for me if I were in this situation, Alyson thought. *You always want to make a great first impression on new people and Gina deserves that much as she heads over to meet the new staff that would be taking care of her.*

Alyson never forgot this experience, which has helped to mold her into the nurse that she is today. Every day since then she has applied these philosophies to her nursing practice.

Massachusetts General Hospital (MGH) is on the next block, literally across the street from Shriners. It is one of only a few level I adult burn units in this area of the country, and the care I received by the entire medical staff was second to none. Dr. Schultz and Dr. Ryan were my doctors.

As soon as I arrived I was sent up to the ICU under the care of the MGH Burn Associates on the thirteenth floor of the hospital. Infection and high fever continued to plague me, however, and I was placed in an "incubation room" inside a sterile oxygen tent with three other burn patients, all in comas, all in oxygen tents. It must have seemed like something out of a bad science fiction movie for my family. For two weeks, before I was put into a regular room in the Burn Unit, when my family would come in to visit me they'd wind up talking not only to me but to the other patients in the room, as well.

I had been in an oxygen tent at Shriners for a short period of time, and almost everyone who saw me like this thought of the famous "Bubble Boy" episode from *Seinfeld*. So, they called me The Bubble Girl.

It was hollow laughter, however. My family was nervous about the change of hospitals, as well as the seeming lack of change in my condition. They had gotten use to Shriners. The familiarity with the staff, the doctors, even the setting, was comforting. It was like starting all over again. They didn't know what to expect now. They knew one thing; it would be more difficult to maintain the around-the-clock bedside vigil that they had while I was at Shriners. Since the apartment provided by Shriners was only for families of patients they were treating, my mother and step dad could no longer stay there. They were facing a daily commute, which in and of itself was not the problem. They were afraid that something was going to happen with regard to my condition, good or bad, while they were on I-95, and they did not want to be stuck in traffic when it did.

Shriners provided accommodations for my family for another week, allowing them to stay in the apartment. After that, The Family Resource Fund provided my family with a room at the Holiday Inn close to Massachusetts General so that they were able to continue to be close to me. It was something that I know meant a lot to them. They didn't expect such charity, and seeing as how long I had been hospitalized, they would have gone bankrupt to be close to me and would not have thought twice about it. There were many saving graces for me personally during this time, and this was just another example.

My friend Trish acted as a liaison between my department and my family. These people also provided and collected food donations for my sons, who were in school and trying to resume a schedule as close to a normal as possible. This was not charity, it was love, and it made a very difficult time for Alex and Nicholas a little easier. And I'll never forget it.

It was at this time during my stay at Mass General that my family encountered a person who had a profound effect on them and also put them immediately at ease with my medical change of venue. This individual was a male nurse named Richard. He was as personable as he was positive, and he always had a cheery anecdote or a joke to share. Garbed in special decontaminated clothing, he used to climb right inside this clear plastic environment which kept me safe from germs in purified air. He would talk right to my face, whispering softly into my ear, telling me stories, reassuring me that I was going to be okay. Sometimes he would do this for hours. Many people believe that you can hear and experience the world even while in a coma. Richard certainly believed it. He said that a familiar voice, speaking in a gentle tone helps to reassure the patient and ease their anxiety.

My family already had an understanding of this principle, and would talk to me often. But it was difficult for them, and made them uneasy. Up until then, they would tell me things, like how I was going to be ok, but this was largely to make themselves feel better. Richard showed them that our voices were benefiting me.

He felt comfortable with my family, and they became very close to him. Seeing the positive energy Richard conveyed, my family quickly adopted his approach and began talking to me all the time. They couldn't go inside "the bubble," of course, but my family grew to trust Richard so much that they would tell him things that they wanted to have whispered directly into my ears.

At one point, Matt, asked him, "Tell Gina not to leave us." He jokingly added, "She can't leave me alone with her sister. She'll be an absolute nightmare. *You can't leave me, Gina.*"

The same week that my family was adjusting to my transfer to Mass General, lawyers from around the region descended upon the memorialized ruins of The Station nightclub after being granted legal access. Superior Court Judge Alice Gibney, who had been assigned to oversee all the pretrial proceedings for the pending civil lawsuits, gave the litigators *carte blanche* access to the ruins all day. The judge was also on the site to handle any discord that might arise.

In a bit of irony, the personal injury lawyers could only step onto the grounds if they first signed a liability release holding the town and the realty company that owned the property harmless from any injuries they might suffer while rummaging through the debris. You wonder if they were chuckling to themselves when they signed the documents.

These on-site inspections were part of the pretrial discovery process for the pending civil litigation.

It would seem rather unlikely that there would be anything of substance left to pick through, especially when considering that everything of any value had already been collected and removed by investigators conducting the criminal aspect of the investigation. As it turned out, there wasn't much for the lawyers to do except to snap photographs and take various measurements. It was part of a process. For personal injury lawyers, the devil is in the details. And as anyone who was at The Station that night can attest, the devil himself was in the fire. If they looked hard enough, they might just find hoof prints in the ashes.

In April, the owners of The Station, who had been keeping a low profile, were back in the news when the state Department of Labor and Training ordered the Derderians to pay $1.66 million for failing to carry worker's compensation for their employees. It was the maximum fine allowed by the law for failure to carry the mandatory insurance: $1,000 per day for 1,066 days. It was also the largest penalty ever imposed in Rhode Island.

Jeffrey B. Pine, former R. I. Attorney General and legal counsel representing Jeffrey Derderians at that time, believed that this fine was excessive and had been imposed because of the extreme emotional toll that The Station fire had on the state. Pine called the fine excessive, and cited that even repeat and longtime offenders had not been fined the maximum amount. Other death cases, he mentioned, hadn't received nearly as much as the Derderians. Pine promised to appeal the ruling.

By law, employers are responsible to their employees to make the workplace safe. However, accidents can happen even when every reasonable safety measure has been taken. To protect employers from lawsuits resulting from workplace accidents and to provide medical care and compensation for lost income to employees hurt in workplace accidents, in almost every state, businesses are required to buy workers compensation insurance. In Rhode Island, businesses with one or more employees are required to carry worker's compensation.

Workers compensation insurance covers workers injured on the job, whether they're hurt on the workplace premises or elsewhere, or in auto accidents while on business. It also covers work-related illnesses.

Workers compensation provides payments to injured workers, without regard to who was at fault in the accident, for time lost from work and for medical and rehabilitation services. It also provides death benefits to surviving spouses and dependents.

The Station owners broke the law by operating their business without workers' compensation insurance from the time they bought the establishment in March 2000 until it burnt to the ground on February 20, 2003. Criminal charges for this illegality were being considered at that time by the State Attorney General's office. Four employees were killed in the fire, and if the Derderians had purchased the required insurance, then the families of these employees would have received $15,000 for burial expenses, as well as a portion of their lost wages. Also, the other employees who were injured or hospitalized as a result of the fire would have received compensation for lost wages and medical care. Instead, because of the Derderians knowingly went without the insurance, their employees got nothing.

Later in April, it was announced that several benefit concerts were being organized to pay tribute to Great White guitarist Ty Longley, who was among the victims of The Station Fire. This was not something a majority of the families wanted to hear about. It was nothing against Longley, and some could look at it as the band just taking care of their own, but a lot of people hold Great White responsible, at least in part, for the fire that killed and injured so many. It was just hard to accept that these guys were going to take the stage again and perform in front of an audience.

On April 29, Great White was scheduled to perform one song as part of a multi-band benefit concert for the Ty Longley Memorial Fund at the Key Club in West Hollywood. The fund had been established by Longley's parents to provide financial assistance to the guitarist's unborn son, victim relief funds and students seeking art scholarships. Heidi Peralta, Longely's girlfriend, was pregnant with their first child. It's sad and tragic that the child will have to grow up without his father. Even more tragic is the sad fact that a total of 64 children lost one or both of their parents in The Station fire.

At that time, Great White also announced that the band had no other plans to play together in the near future. This was good news for many. Two other independent tribute concerts were scheduled, however one in London on April 19 which the band wound not attend and another at the Hard Rock Cafe in Beverly Hills on April 17, where members of Great White would be in the audience.

A number of artists who had collaborated with Longley for a solo album donated the track to an upcoming Ty Longley benefit record *Ty Longley: Regular Guy.* The CD, scheduled for release in May, included two live songs by Great White, an acoustic track by

Jack Russell and songs by 5 Cent Shine and other bands. A full Great White tribute album was also said to be in the works.

It was all unsettling news that came at a bad time. There may have been no good time with regard to any news relating to Great White.

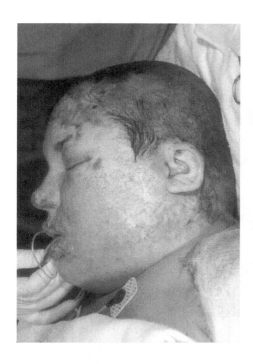

Barely recognizable
after the fire.

December, 2003

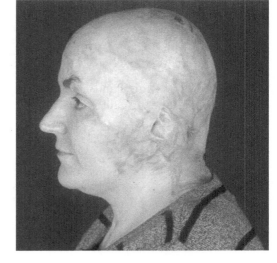

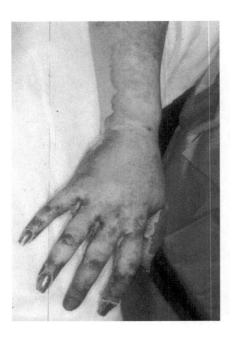

Right hand,
February 23, 2003

Right hand,
December 15, 2003

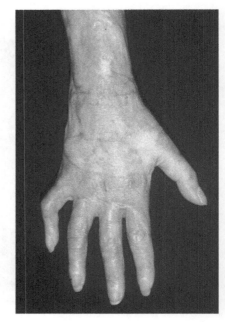

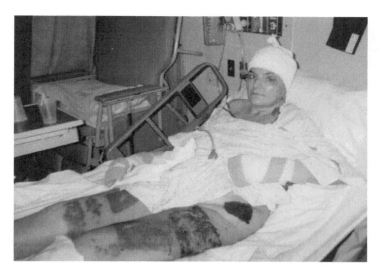

May 19, 2003, with skin harvesting
donor sites clearly visible

With Fred, July 30, 2002

With my sons, Alex and Nicholas
Thanksgiving 2009

With my husband, Steve

CHAPTER 7   AWAKENING

Once in my own room at Massachusetts General Hospital, I settled into a routine of debridement, skin grafts and scar revision surgeries on my hands and fingers.

At various points, I don't know if the level of medication dripping into my veins fluctuated during the course of my coma, but it seemed that at times I drifted closer to consciousness and awareness. Dreams and reality seemed to overlap, much like regular sleep. My family observed this, as well. During this time my left eye had been bandaged, but my right was not. Occasionally, my stepfather noticed that my right eye would pop open suddenly when a male voice spoke. He believed this was because I was looking and listening for Fred.

I can't say if that was true or not, but I did experience moments of partial awareness. I recall hearing indistinct conversations between my doctors and nurses as well as the voices of my family talking to me and one another.

I was still very much unconscious, deeply medicated and technically in a coma, so I didn't see anything, catching glimpses of images that were only in my head. There was never any pain or fear that I recall. No angst of any kind. Just awareness. Time had no relevance.

It was very strange.

Then, as March rolled around the doctors began to wean me slowly off the medication that was keeping me in a comatose state in order to bring me back to consciousness. This was when the hallucinations were most vivid, most bizarre. I've never taken LSD or any other psychedelic drugs, but I imagine this transitional state of consciousness through which I was passing would have been comparable.

I remember some of these dreams clearly, like the one dream being in my sister's SUV, which was parked outside a pizzeria. I was a passenger, but Stephanie was not in the vehicle with me. She left me inside. I'm not sure what this means, but perhaps it represents how alone I felt since the fire, no matter who else was around me. What's even more strange is that Donovan Williams, a

Station Fire survivor who was comatose in the room across the hall from mine, later told me that he had exactly the same dream. So maybe it was just our families talking out loud about ordering a pizza, which we overheard.

There were other examples like this, but by far the most bizarre of these was a recurring hallucination I had of this naked man in my room. He wasn't even attractive, just some ugly naked man. He was very scary, besides the nakedness. He would just be standing there, with a psychotic look on his face. Sometimes he would be in the room when my family was there, but they never saw him. It was frustrating. He was there even after I had regained consciousness. The trach was still in my throat but I would try to draw everyone's attention to the indecent intruder, mouthing that there was an ugly naked man in the room and pointing to him. They could read my lips, but of course could not see the man. They didn't realize that I had been hallucinating, and became concerned, believing that someone had entered my room during the night. They even called a nurse to find out if anyone could have gotten in my room. We still laugh about it today, but at the time it was spooky.

I have no idea how that hallucination might have manifested itself, but I had seen other people in my room who could not possibly have been there, either, including my grandmother who had passed away two years before, and my dad. Two of my grandmother's cousins, who we used to visit in Brooklyn when I was a kid, I had also seen in my room. Dead family members seemed to always be around me, but this was strangely comforting.

Coming out of a coma is not like in the movies, where one moment a person seems to be in a deep sleep, eyes closed, and then suddenly their eyes pop open and they're instantly aware. My eyes eventually did open and awareness seeped in, but it was very gradual.

The last dream that I had I can still remember clearly.

I was sitting on a carousel, smiling, happy. I've always loved merry-go-rounds, ever since I was a kid. I'd go on them as an adult all the time, and never felt foolish or silly. In my dream, there were many other people on the ride, and I didn't know anyone. They were just indistinct figures rising up and down all around me. Suddenly, the carousel caught fire, and I realized that I could not escape. Round and round we went, and it was getting hotter and blacker. Then I heard a voice. I realized that it was the person directly in front of me, telling me, "I'm going to get you out. I'm going to save you."

In my dream, I didn't distinguish the gender of the speaker. However, the identity of the person that promised to save me from this dream world fire was revealed to me shortly after I had awakened from my coma. The man who pulled me off the burning carousel was Dr. Michael Finley, a psychologist who had been appointed to me by the hospital. As soon as I met him I knew he was the one. It was pretty amazing. If spotting the person who pulled me out of The Station as it was burning was that easy, that would be a real trick. I wish I could just look at someone and know who saved my life for real.

What I do know is what I saw the first time I opened my eyes and had a conscious memory.

Matt had some business in Boston this day, and he stopped by the hospital to visit. He saw that my eyes were open, but this was something my family had seen many times in recent weeks. My eyes would suddenly pop open and even begin to tear as they were talking to me, making them think that I was awake. Whoever was in my room at the time would get all excited, alert the doctors and call the rest of the family. But I was never awake. This had gotten them a few times already, so Matt knew that my eyes being open now didn't mean that I could see anything, and it certainly didn't mean that I was awake. This time, he didn't think anything of it at first, but soon he realized that my eyes had been open for a long time. They usually close quite quickly. Not only that, but he could see that my eyes were tracking him when he moved and spoke.

I'll never forget seeing Matt's face staring down at me for a moment before yelling ecstatically, "She's awake! OH MY GOD! SHE'S REALLY AWAKE!"

My first thoughts and words were Alex and Nicholas. Matt told me that the boys were fine. He said that Alex had a baseball game that day, but that didn't make any sense to me. I had been in a coma for eleven weeks, but I thought it was the next day, and I know you can't play baseball in February, not in Rhode Island, anyway.

I then asked about Fred, and did not get any response from Matt.

I did not actually speak. The trach was still in my throat which made speech impossible. So I mouthed the words and my brother-in-law read my lips.

I had no recollection of the fire at first. I didn't know it was almost three months since I was last conscious. I didn't know Fred was gone. I was still in a bubble, figuratively.

I knew I was in a hospital, but I didn't know why, and they didn't tell me anything about that right away either.

During this time, I recalled being extremely scared. I was frightened all the time. It was like waking up from a horrible nightmare that you can't remember. I felt disconnected from the world. However, some of the earliest events stick out most in my mind. I remember the first time I met my lawyers.

Matt came into my room to visit me with two men and introduced them as my lawyers, Al Gemma and Mark Mandell. My brother-in-law had contacted the Providence law firm of Mandell, Schwartz & Boisclair, LTD to ensure that my rights were represented during any criminal or civil trial that might result from the fire and the injuries I sustained.

It was actually Mark Mandell who first asked me if I had any recollections of the fire.

"What fire?" I said.

He told me that I had been at The Station when the nightclub caught fire. Then it all came back to me, and with extraordinary vividness, as if it was happening to me right then. The searing heat and the flames, the horrible screaming, the people with their heads on fire. These haunting images assaulted my senses all over again and I began to cry.

Mark later told me that the look on my face, one of abject terror, when I reacted to this question was the reason why he became so deeply involved with Station Fire victims.

I remembered being trapped inside The Station as it burned and thinking I was going die there. Now it made sense. I had survived the fire and was in the hospital recovering.

My concern then turned to Fred.

I remembered Fred guiding me through the smoke, trying to get us outside. He was pushing me toward the exit, and then I lost him in the crowd as we tried to escape.

Naturally, my next question was, "Where's Fred?" But nobody wanted to tell me. In fact, anytime I would ask about him, and I did over and over for a long time, they would pretend to be unable to decipher what I was mouthing. They would just change the subject, telling me instead about Alex and Nicholas and how well they were doing.

So I remained blissfully ignorant that he was dead. For a while, anyway. Everyone wanted me to remain positive so that I would be able to focus all my energy into my healing and recuperation. Having survived this long and emerging from a coma were accomplishments to build on, and my doctors and family didn't want to me to experience any sort of setback at this point. They kept telling me not to worry about Alex and Nicholas. The boys would be fine. I was assured that everything would be taken care of. And it was. All I had to do was get better.

The first thing my lawyer did was ask my doctor to draft and sign a letter indicating that I had been a victim of The Station Fire. The document was needed to protect my assets and keep any creditors from my door. Mark Mandell informed me that he planned on moving forward in a more methodical manner, rather than rushing to court to file a lawsuit like so many attorneys for other Station fire survivors and families were doing at that time. Before filing a suit on my behalf, he wanted to be sure that all possible defendants had been identified. He had hired his own fire experts to exhaustively examine the evidence that had been collected so that nothing was missed.

The filing of my claim was slowed the following month when my lawyer discovered that, according to Rhode Island State Law, before a suit can be filed against a town, an administrative claim had to first be filed with the Town Council. The town would then have forty days to attempt to settle the claim. After that time, if no settlement attempt is made, the lawsuit can then be filed. So the administrative claim was made on my behalf and on the behalf of my children.

Pursuant to Section 45-15-5 of the General Laws of Rhode Island, notice was given to the city of West Warwick that my injuries and losses stemming from the Station Fire were sustained due to the negligence and egregious negligence of the municipality of the town of West Warwick, its agents, servants and employees in the performance and/or failure to perform governmental and proprietary functions. Ten specific instances were cited, including failure to adequately inspect The Station nightclub for safety hazards and violations and failure to enforce fire safety laws, regulations and standards.

In the days immediately following my return to consciousness, the fear did not leave. It stayed with me. I definitely did not want to sleep. I had done enough of that, and I was terrified that I would not wake up this time. Everyone was careful not to include particulars about the fire. I did not know there had been any deaths at all. Everything led me to believe that some people had been injured like me, and that Fred must be in another hospital.

During this time, my family began to fill me in on some of the details of my injury and the process that I had undergone to get to this point. That was chilling in itself. When my mother described how I was transferred from Shriners, she told me they had wheeled me down a long corridor, and I actually recalled seeing this exact image as it happened. I've never been a person who had a strong believe in the supernatural, or anything of that nature. However, during my period of unconsciousness, besides my dad and my deceased grandmother and her cousins, I felt that Fred was with me in spirit, though I didn't know he had died in the fire. All this sensory input was like something in a dream that seems so real until you wake up.

But some of these things *were* real. Real events. Real sounds. Voices, which penetrated the medication and the coma. The sound of construction that I heard in my slumber. There really was construction going on outside my window while at was at Mass General.

At one point, Matt was sitting beside my bed when I turned to him and whispered, "I guess I didn't leave you." I don't know why I said that, but he just looked at me amazement and asked me if I had heard what he said weeks earlier about not leaving him alone with Stephanie because she would be an emotional wreck without me. I was still deep in coma when he said this, and I couldn't say that now I had a conscious recollection of him telling me that, but my words to him could only have been a response to his earlier remarks.

Such strange experiences were not just confined to the girl in the bed, however. They also happened to people who were at my bedside. My sister, for example, later told me that while I was in a semiconscious state I asked her, *Where's the baby? What happened to the baby?* Realizing I was in the hospital, I probably thought I was there to deliver a baby. I had been in a hospital only two times before, when I gave birth to Alex and Nicholas. Stephanie asked me if I was pregnant, and when my eyes grew wide and teary with excitement in response, she actually became convinced. It's funny now, and we joke about it occasionally because she actually had the doctors give me a pregnancy test to be sure. It was negative, of course.

I cannot thank my family enough for all that they did. Just as the doctors were keeping my body alive and functioning, my family became surrogates to every other aspect of my life. My mother and my sister manifested emotional strength and comfort when I needed it most while my brother-in-law kept the paper trail of my life flowing. In many ways Matt took on the role of my personal manager. He did so much for me and my sons, taking care of the business matters of my life that I could not attend to myself, including my finances and making sure my bills were paid. He kept that part of my life on track.

When things were at their most dire for me, Stephanie and Matt had actually been preparing to become full-time legal guardians for my children. They did this without a moment's hesitation, and there was no other couple I could see raising my boys. Early on, my mom filed a Certificate of Appointment with the Probate Court so that she would be recognized as my temporary guardian. The appointment was approved while I was still in a coma, and she was given the responsibility of making all legal decisions for me and on my behalf of my children while I was incapacitated.

As my legal representative, one of the first things that my mother did was request that the Social Security Benefits for Alex and Nicholas be paid to her as my representative payee. She also signed my disability benefit claim through Liberty Mutual, the insurance company of my employer at Rhode Island Hospital. The boys were all that mattered, and it was important that they not be deprived of anything during this time. As it was, they were temporarily deprived of their mother, but they were not lacking the love of family and the caring of an entire community who were all there for them when I was not.

After the fire, my family proved over and over again just how much they cared and loved me. It was amazing. I'll never forget it.

And I can never pay them back. I am so fortunate to be blessed with such a great family.

My coworkers also continued to be confident and supportive throughout my ordeal, maintaining great hope for my recovery. Trish provided frequent updates of my medical condition to Margaret Prendergast, who shared my progress reports on flyers she distributed throughout the hospital. The news that I was conscious for the first time since the night of the fire reached many people almost instantly. When I emerged from the coma everyone in my department cheered and prayed for my continued improvement.

The fact that I had gotten as far as I did and was making progress was an achievement that others could share in, and it was such a good feeling to know that my efforts were making other people happy.

There were four doctors that I was working for in the Pediatric Cardiology Group, along with a clinic secretary who handled the patients that came in. They all believed in me. My employers kept my job open for me for however long my recovery and rehabilitation took. The department hired temps to assist while I was out. I so grateful for the way everyone stuck by me and never gave up.

All this only made me want to continue to improve and recover to the point where I could return to work and take care of my family. It would be the best way to thank everyone for what they had done for me the last three months.

I had no way of knowing what I was in for, however. Waking up from a coma was just the beginning of a long struggle to regain anything close to the life that I had once known.

CHAPTER 8   LOSS AND RECOVERY

I was connected to a feeding tube, and my mouth was so dry that it hurt. The wet sponge just wasn't doing it. I was begging everyone for something to drink, it didn't matter what it was, but the doctors wouldn't allow even water because they could not be sure of the extent of the damage to my lungs and there was a danger that I would aspirate the liquid directly into my lungs. It was considered a sign of progress when I began to eat ice chips and applesauce, a food I never liked. It was even warm, but it was wet and I ate it like it was the most delectable tiramisu you could ever imagine.

They had also begun to remove my trach for longer and longer periods of time. At this point, it became impossible for my family to stall any longer when I asked about Fred. Someone had to tell me, and it was my sister who finally broke the news to me.

One morning, I asked again what hospital Fred was in and everyone in my room paused.

Even with the trach removed, I could barely speak above a whisper, but they could clearly hear me. The second time I asked I made sure I enunciated each word slowly and carefully.

"Where's Fred?" I asked again

Tears were rolling down my sister's face before she said anything. Then she just told me.

"He didn't make it out of the building," she said.

"What? Where's Fred?"

"He died in the fire, Gina. I'm so sorry."

"No. It's not true. Nobody died."

"Oh, no. Ninety-nine people died, Gina. It wasn't just Fred."

I went completely numb. Too shocked to even cry at first. I couldn't comprehend that so many people had been killed in the fire. Then it slowly settled in my brain, the sobering fact that Fred was one of the victims.

The heartache that followed was in many ways more unendurable than any of the physical pain I would experience as a result of my burns. And there wasn't a doctor on earth who was going to be able to fix that pain.

A devastating feeling of dread overwhelmed me and I just lost it. Just as the fire had consumed my body, the news of Fred's death destroyed everything that was inside me. I started to cry and I didn't think I was ever going to stop. I wanted to die right then and there, and I would have been happy to do so. If I could not be with Fred, I had nothing to live for. That was my initial response. A psychiatrist was summoned to my bedside. That pain lasted for a long time. I couldn't even begin to say how long I just tuned out my life, like a radio dial stuck between two stations. It got worse before it got better.

My family never gave up on me. They kept telling me that I had to get well for my Alex and Nicholas, for myself, and for Fred, who would not want me to give up. It took a while for me to see that they were right. They told me all along that there was a reason I had survived, and eventually I came to believe that. Even if it was only to keep Fred's memory alive, then there *was* a purpose for my recovery. And that's what I decided to do. It didn't happen at the hospital. It didn't happen until much later, after the rehabilitation, after I had been home, after a lengthy adjustment period.

Recovering became a mission. I don't think I could have done it without Fred. He saved me that night of the fire, and his memory sustained me and kept me alive after, giving me the will to continue to live the rest of my life.

Besides struggling with depression early on, I battled a couple bouts of pneumonia. As my lungs cleared, I began using an incentive spirometer to build up my pulmonary capacity. Soon I was sitting up and trying to stand. And now that I was awake I had to endure one of the most harrowing experiences imaginable for the first time in a conscious state: debridement. Even with the painkillers, it was horrible. Having gone through it, it's not something I would wish on anyone. Every time the nurses would come in my heart would sink and I would get sick to my stomach because I knew what I was in for. They began by changing my dressings. Many times I would already be crying in anticipation of the pain. From head to toe they would unwrap me. It took about two hours. The bandages did not come off easily. Chunks of dead and dying skin peeled off with it and I would scream out each time another piece of me was ripped from my body. Then they would clean me, gently washing away the remaining flecks of black, dried flesh in the warm bath water. Getting wrapped back up in fresh sterile bandages felt good. It was comforting and it took a fraction of the time that it did to remove them, but it was short-lived. The whole process lasted about three hours, and it was repeated two or three times a day. It was sheer torture, but I thought of Fred and my family willing me through this and I was somehow able to endure it.

Up to this point, I had not seen my reflection in a mirror, and I had no desire to do so. *What difference would it make anyway*, I thought. I lost Fred, and it didn't matter much to me then what I looked like under the bandages. From what I *could* see, it appeared that my hands were in the worst shape. However, from the attention and time it took to change the bandages on my head, I thought I must have looked truly frightful.

While I had managed to avoid my own reflection, I could not help but notice the other patients on the floor who had also suffered burn injuries. Being in a burn unit, that's all you see. There was one woman I would see walk by my room all the time. Her face was badly burnt and I just assumed that I looked the same way. I was sure that if I looked in a mirror I would see her face staring back at me. It was after I had seen this woman for the first time that I asked my nurse to remove all the mirrors from room. I didn't even want to see my reflection by accident.

I really had no idea as to the extent of the physical changes to my body until about a week after my awakening when a nurse came in my room to change my dressings. In fact, it was the day after my sister told me that Fred had died, so I was not in the best of moods. The nurse's name was Edna, and she had always been tender and compassionate with me, like everyone else that I came in contact with at the hospital.

First she unwrapped my head, which was basically an open wound, and then coated my scalp with silver sulfadiazine, a topical antibacterial cream. This was a clear fluid, and looked exactly like water while it was inside the bottle. The moment it was touched by air, however, it turned black. It dried on my head and became hard, like an eggshell, and then it was ready to be picked off a piece at a time. The burned and dead layers of skin would adhere to the substance and were removed in the process.

While Edna was doing this to my scalp that day, she told me not to worry, that they would be able to rebuild my ear.

I didn't know what she was talking about, and I said, "My ear? What do you mean?" I was thinking that there couldn't be anything wrong with either one of my ears because I could hear fine.

"You didn't know you lost your ear?"

I couldn't believe it. I didn't know what to say.

Edna must have seen the bewildered and frightened look on my face. She felt so bad she walked out of the room crying. Just outside the door, my mother was waiting. Edna explained to her what she had said. My mother told her it was okay, and when she came back into the room she apologized profusely to me. I tried to reassure her myself, telling her that it wasn't like it was secret, one that I would not find out about at some point. I wasn't mad at her. She didn't know. But I was very troubled by this sudden revelation, enough to ask to speak to my doctor, who later came in, again with a psychiatrist that he toted around with him like a personal bodyguard whenever he spoke to me lately.

With my voice shaking with agitation and fear, I demanded that he tell me if I had lost anything besides my ear. Part of me didn't want to know. I just didn't want any more surprises. I wasn't sure I could take the sudden shock of another loss, even one as seemingly insignificant as an ear, which I can assure you it is not.

The doctor told me that, yes, I had lost my left ear, but I had not lost anything else. He explained the severity of the burns to my head and the consequences of the fourth degree burns to scalp, including the likelihood that I would never grow my own hair. He told me they had cosmetically saved my hands, which were still wrapped, and cautioned me that I would probably never use them again the way I had before.

He told me this as if it had been carved on stone tablets brought down from Mt. Sinai, and if I accepted it as truth, the consequences were much more significant than my burned ear. As a secretary, my hands were my job, but if they were damaged as badly as he said then there was a possibility that I might never work again. I knew there was no way I could *not* go back to work. They couldn't take that away from me, too. I wouldn't let them. The doctor said that he had saved my hands, and as long as I still had them I was determined that I would use them. I didn't care how long it took. I made the determination right then and there that I would work again.

As far as my lower body was concerned, he said that my legs were fine except for a small third degree burn on one knee, which should heal on its own. The front and back of my legs, however, were a patchwork of scars because this was one of the areas that had been used, and would continue to be used, as donor sites for skin grafting procedures.

Only portions of my back, he informed me, were severely burned. The unusual pattern of the burns was suggestive that untouched areas of my body may have been protected from the heat and flames by the bodies of other victims lying across me.

I could not help thinking that one of them may have been Fred. It was an unbearable thought and I tried to push it away, but I couldn't. My mother told me that my clothes had been recovered relatively intact while I wound up in the hospital with severe burns. Likewise, the earrings that I wore that night survived the fire even though my left ear did not. Fred had given me the earrings, as well as a ring and bracelet that I had been wearing. I still have these items today, but I will only wear the ring.

After the doctor left, I felt completely depleted of energy and empty inside. I had woken from a three-month coma and within a week I had learned that I had been in a massive fire that had killed a hundred people, including my fiancé, and I had been badly burnt, had lost an ear and would have to undergo numerous surgeries and intensive rehabilitation before I will be able to go home.

I had been crying for a week straight. Now, in all my despair, I could not get my eyes to tear, nor could I get them to close. If I slept at all that night, it was with my eyes wide open and staring at the ceiling.

There were so many questions that needed answers, about the fire, the victims, Fred, my sons, but I was in no state of mind, or body, to grapple with them now. Like everything else in my life, it would all have to be put on hold until I was well enough.

One thing was certain, during the seemingly endless and tormenting process of healing, it became very difficult for me to concentrate on anything because of the excruciating pain. It hurt just to move a finger. The skin, as it healed, grew back uneven, discolored and stiff. The new tissue was stretched so tight, especially around my joints and fingers, that it made all my movements slow and deliberate. Calcium was building up in many of my joints, severely limiting my mobility and maximizing the discomfort. Touching or being touched became an unpleasant experience. Aggressive therapy and surgery were the only ways for me to get my body back.

Although I had miraculously survived the fire, I was still a very long way from being able to do the things I wanted to do, like be at home, go to work, play with my kids. I wasn't sure I would ever be able to do any of them again no matter what I did. So psychological counseling became a part of my recovery and every bit as important as the physical therapy that lay ahead.

I realized that I would be forever scarred despite the numerous skin grafts and reconstructive surgeries I had undergone and would undergo in the future. I would never be able to grow my own hair, another permanent reminder of what I had gone through, losing so much of myself in the fire that night.

I remember being told by doctors not to expect too much. This scared me. I thought they were telling me that I would be this way forever. It made me mad, and I began lashing out at anyone who walked in my room. The Pope himself could have come in to visit me and I would not have wanted to see him either. Like the pontiff, however, everyone seemed to understand. I was the only one who didn't understand it. That's why I was angry. I felt helpless, even though I wasn't. I didn't know how much control I actually had over my whole recovery.

At the same time, as bad as my injuries were, after hearing about some of the horrendous injuries that other victims had sustained, I did not feel I had any right to complain. I was alive, at least. I should be happy about that.

Shouldn't I?

Then something happened that helped me to realize just how fortunate I had been, how fortunate my family had been. That event happened shortly after I was transferred from Massachusetts General Hospital to Spaulding Rehabilitation Hospital to begin my physical therapy program. Before I left, the mother of Pamela Gruttadauria, a survivor who was also in MGH, came to visit me in my room. During the course of our stay there together, my mother had gotten to know Pamela's mom. She wanted to say good-bye to us. I was being prepared for my transfer to Spaulding when Pam's mother told me that when this was all over her daughter and I were going to become good friends and that we would have a party to celebrate. Sadly, despite her mother's optimism, Pamela died of multiple organ failure due to infection several days later. She and her family had endured so much, including numerous surgeries and a constant battle with infections. One of the most severely burned survivors, Pamela's hands had to be removed and her eyes sewn shut. She had been on a ventilator and heavily sedated since the fire. She had never fully regained consciousness during the seventy-three days since she was pulled out of the fire before succumbing to her injuries on May 4, 2003.

I remember being devastated by the news of Pamela's death. Not only was it sad for her mother and the rest of her family, but it was terrifying for me. She became the one-hundredth and final victim of The Station fire, but at the time nobody knew if there would be any more. And I didn't know if I would be the next one. I couldn't help constantly thinking that every conscious moment might be my last. If it could happen to Pam, it could happen to me. Psychologically, this concern stayed with me for a long time. During this time I was dealing with my younger son, Nick, who was still afraid to come near me. When he came into my room, he would hide somewhere or stand behind someone the entire time. If I suddenly died, the last thing he would remember was being scared of his mother, and I would never get to kiss him or hold him in my arms one last time.

Pam's death made me think even more about what was going to become of my sons, and how my injuries were going to impact their futures.

What have I done to them? I thought.

Nick was only in first grade, and at the same time that he was worried about losing his mother, he was also dealing with the possible loss of a classmate. A little girl, who he just adored, had a brain tumor and was not doing well. I could not help him or comfort him because he was so afraid of me that he would not come near me. It was too much tragedy to deal with at such a tender age. How could all this not have a negative impact on his emotional well-being?

Even my oldest son, Alex, I worried about. He was somewhat of a hyperactive kid, and school was enough of a struggle for him.

I thought this would take his focus completely away from studying and his life would be ruined all because of me.

As it turned out, I didn't give Alex and Nick enough credit. I'm so proud of them. They are two truly amazing kids.

CHAPTER 9   REHABILITATION

When I left Massachusetts General for Spaulding, I still needed oxygen. I was also having some difficulty breathing and I was still coughing up viscous black soot from my lungs through my trach. Despite these problems, the doctors believed I was stable enough to make the transition and begin my rehabilitation.

I didn't feel ready, however. At least not psychologically. I was petrified to leave Mass General. In the short time I was awake I had come to trust everyone there with my life, now I was going somewhere else and I was expected to put my faith in a whole new set of strangers. They would have to perform very intimate functions for me that I was still not capable of doing for myself. I felt like a child who was being adopted. Something that I had no control over. The only thing I could think to do to try to make the transition easier was to take someone with me. I remember telling Edna, the nurse in the burn unit, that she had to come with me. I didn't want anyone else changing my bandages. I couldn't imagine anyone else touching me. I had gotten so used to Edna and some of the other nurses at MGH that a bond had formed between us just as strong as a mother and a child. The separation anxiety was real.

The day before my discharge, a lot of my family came to visit me, including my cousin Debbie, who I've always been as close to as a sister. During a rare quiet moment, she took me aside and whispered, "When you were in a coma, I prayed to God to let you live, and if he did that I told him I would give up ten years of my life."

I didn't know what to say, but that is a pretty big IOU. I gave her a big hug and a kiss. That was a start.

My Uncle Joe and Aunt Anna were there as well, and they happened to be in my room at the same time that one of the nurses came in to paint my toes. I was taken by surprise. After all these people did for me, now they were going to paint my toes?

"You cannot leave Mass General without feeling pretty," the nurse told me.

My uncle, who is as friendly and as fun-loving a guy as you will ever meet, asked her to paint his pinky fingernail. But he wasn't joking about that. He told her that he would not wash it off until the day I got home from rehab. She painted his right pinky and he kept his word.

My Aunt Anna had recently been laid off from her work, and she looked at this as a blessing in disguise because she spent much of that time helping my parents and my sons, the people who are most important to me. That day, more than any other, showed how strong of a family unit we were.

Beyond my cousin Debbie, Uncle Joe and Aunt Anna, there are so many family members whose love and support I am thankful for. They were all there for me and my two boys.

So off I went to Spaulding to begin aggressive physical and occupational therapy programs. It was here that I experienced some of the worst pain of the entire ordeal. It was such a demoralizing pain that I began to question if mobility was worth enduring such agony. Like my early debridement experience, just seeing my therapist entering the room would start me crying. I remember thinking that if my therapist saw me in such distress she might feel bad and not put me through the rigors of therapy that day. It never worked.

None of this was any reflection on the facility, its chief medical officer, Dr. Joel Stein, or my physical therapist, Kristen Forget.

Throughout a rehabilitation that was fraught with enormous challenges and difficulty, Kristen was at once demanding and encouraging. She was a joy to be around, something that certainly could not be said of me during this time of my life. She was trying to get the best out of me when I was at my worst.

Each day would begin with some stretching in bed, which sounds easy enough, but it was not. It was pure torture. I had been in bed for so long without moving that my muscles had atrophied considerably. I was extremely weak. I had lost so much weight from inactivity and having survived on a liquid diet of intravenous fluid for three months that just shifting my body in bed so that my stiff legs were hanging over the side was an accomplishment.

The first time I did this, Kristen asked me to put my legs down, and I told her that I couldn't, my knee joints were frozen.

To get me off the bed and onto my feet, they had to rock me from side to side, like a large bureau being moved across a bedroom floor. When I finally *was* standing, I could not bear weight on my legs for more than a couple of seconds at a time. I tired immediately and became dizzy all at once. A couple of times I nearly fainted. It was frightening. I began to wonder if I would ever walk again.

Heterotrophic ostification was the consequence of my lack of movement for such a prolonged period of time. The inactivity caused calcium to build up in my knees, locking them in place. Without muscle strength or the ability to bend my knees, walking was out of the question. It was Kristen's job to see to it that I overcame these obstacles so that I would one day walk again.

She had always been honest with me. She told me that the calcium problem would present the greatest challenge for me. And unfortunately, there was only one way for me to gain my flexibility back, and that to have my stiff knees bent manually in order to break up the calcium deposits that were encasing the joints. Every time she worked on my knees I felt, and heard, the crunch of the calcium grinding and breaking in her hands. It was a terrifying sound to have to listen to, especially after I was told that a danger existed whereby chunks of calcium could become dislodged and relocate in other joints, traveling up to my hips or down to my ankles, feet and toes.

My right elbow had affected by the same condition, only far worse. There was evidence that it had already begun progressing up my arm toward my shoulder joint, and would later require several surgeries to properly correct.

Long before I thought it would happen, I was taking small steps with a walker. I was always unsure of myself, thinking I was going to fall and hurt myself, even with Kristen standing right beside me.

I'll never forget the morning she came into my room and took the walker away from me.

"Ok," she said. "You're not going to need this anymore. Now you're going to do it without the walker."

She was determined to have me walking again. She was confident about it, too. I could sense that, and I trusted her. She knew what I was feeling and kept reassuring me. She told me that she had never had a patient fall and that I was not going to be the one to break that streak. Because I knew she wasn't going to leave my side, it gave me the confidence to keep trying. And with her help, I did walk again, and much more quickly than I ever would have imagined.

My legs were still very thin and weak, my flexibility limited. My stamina and balance were still a long way off, too, but I was still walking on my own. Though my first steps were small, like a six-month old baby on her feet for the first time, it was quite an accomplishment and I was very proud.

Getting up and down stairs, however, would remain a challenge for some time to come. Walking and climbing with knees with little flexibility are two entirely different motions. Descending was much worse. In the beginning, I would go down backward because it was easier to navigate the steps that way, and it was less dangerous. Climbing in and out of a car, which we simulated in therapy and practiced outside in the parking lot in a real car, presented a similar problem. But I was able to meet all these challenges and conquer them due in large part to Kristen's efforts, as well as the other staff members at Spaulding, including Stephanie, my occupational therapist. Stephanie also played a vital role in my recovery because she was the person who worked closely with me for many days to show me how to perform the tasks that I needed to when I went back to work.

There were two nurses that I will never forget who deserve mention. They also happened to be sisters. Not in the religious sense, they weren't nuns. They had the thickest Irish accents, and I loved them immediately. Their primary job was to change my dressings. It was not a pleasant task for either of them, but they had become instant experts on how to handle patients with severe burns after recently treating two young women at the hospital who had been in a massive electric explosion. These people did much more than help my physical recovery. They made my stay there, a majority of the time, anyway, cheery and happy and helped me keep my sanity by making me laugh during the most difficult time in my life. We became very close. They were good to me, and I liked them despite the agony they put me through.

One Friday, after another long grueling week came to a close, I was rewarded with a Margarita from TGIF's. I enjoyed this immensely. More than the drink itself, which tasted fantastic, the sense of accomplishment I felt and the feeling that all of us were in this together was something special. I could see myself progressing each week because of their efforts. I had come so far, and my next goal was now within reach. Despite the bond that I had developed between the staff at Spaulding, I wanted to go home.

My relationship with my own family, particularly my boys, had been in limbo now going on four months. It was crushing me to be so close now. Alex and Nicholas still came to visit me at the hospital once a week, and it was something I looked forward to. They needed to see me as much as I needed to see them, but seeing their mother in the hospital in my condition was not easy for them. It obviously affected them differently. Alex, being older, was able to handle it a lot better. He would approach me without hesitation and talk to me, let me hold him. Nicholas had a more difficult time with it. He was quiet and tentative. He barely spoke at all. He was still too scared to get close to me. It hurt to see him look at me with such fear and horror, but I understood and I didn't want to let my disappointment and sadness show. I didn't want to make him feel any worse. I was his mother, but I didn't look or act like the mother that he had known. I realized it was going to take some more time for him to get used to the changes and realize that I was still his mom. I didn't know how long it would be, and didn't want to become disappointed by expecting it by any definite time or date.

Then, on Mother's Day, Nicholas shocked me by getting into the hospital bed with me. He actually spoke to me for the first time and started asking me questions. When he hugged me, it was the best gift I could have gotten.

I've already mentioned Fred as having played as important a role as anyone in my rehabilitation. This is not meant to diminish all that my therapists and everyone else did for me. Without them, I would not have been able to regain the movement and freedom that I enjoy today. By the same token, without Fred's spirit, which I felt so strongly during this time, I would not have wanted to recover. I drew my strength from him. During the entire rehab process, I would constantly look up to the heavens and ask Fred to help get me through it. My therapists would hear me talking out loud to him all the time, asking him to give me strength. They must have thought I was nuts, but I did this every day for months and I got through it.

He's the biggest reason why, today, when something to do with the fire comes up, I get involved. It's for Fred. He helped me through so much, and I want to make sure I do everything I can so that he is remembered. He was too wonderful of a person to be forgotten. As long as there is breath in my lungs, Fred will be alive in me and everything I do.

Just when everyone thought Russell and his band were going to hang up their guitars, hair extensions and pyrotechnic bombs, it was announced that the band was making plans to go back out on the road to begin a nationwide concert series to raise money for The Station Family Fund, a non-profit organization founded by fire survivors.

I remember hearing the news of the benefit concerts around the time I had reconnected with my son, Nicholas, on Mother's Day. I was still finding out the details surrounding the fire that night, but the more I learned about it the more angry I became at everyone associated with The Station. The Derderians. The bouncer. And in particular, Jack Russell and Great White. I could see no good whatsoever coming out a concert event involving them. Despite the money that could be raised for the people who needed it, I was appalled that the band members would even show their faces so soon after the fire. As far as I was concerned, it was blood money they were seeking to collect, and it could not be used to either buy their forgiveness or to resurrect the lives that were taken by them. If their little pity tour could be summed up in a few words, the sentiment of the families and survivors would be, *thanks, but no thanks*. If we had it our way, at least, the concerts never would have happened.

On May 22, survivors and family of fire victims were in court to testify before a legislative commission studying the state's fire code. I could not attend, but we were well represented, and within two weeks the 17-member panel studying the fire laws recommended a radical code update, including mandating the requirement of sprinklers in all nightclubs and abolishing the grandfather clause. It was gratifying to hear that something good was already coming from the tragedy. Hopefully, that trend would continue.

Meanwhile, I was forging ahead in my therapy, though my heart just was not into it. I was ready to go home, and had been for some time. It was extremely frustrating. I had made great strides, but I felt I had hit a wall and my recovery could no longer progress by leaps and bounds. At this point, I could get just as much benefit from outpatient therapy and be home at the same time. I was prepared to make my case to the powers that be at the hospital. I was just waiting for the right time to do it. Every Monday, Dr. Joel Stein would come in talk to me about my therapy and progress. Well, I determined that the next Monday, June 9, was going to be the day. I had worked out this whole long speech in my head that I was going to give the doctor, telling him why I thought he should let me go home. Among my points of contention, I was eating solid food and had greatly improved my strength and range of motion.

I never got the chance to say anything, however.

When he walked into my room that day, before I could utter a single word of my well-rehearsed exit strategy, the doctor asked me, "So, are you ready to go home?"

I was so relieved, I forgot everything I was going to say and I began to cry. Even though I continued to have trouble with chairs and stairs and my eyes were still somewhat impaired due to the heat and smoke of the fire, he let me go home. I was over-whelmed. I almost couldn't believe it. It was all I could think about the rest of the week.

It was also on that day that I met Donovan Williams for the first time. He was with his sister and his mother, who were pushing him down the hall in his wheel chair when my step dad and I encountered them. It was literally moments after I found out that I was going home.

My step dad introduced me to Donovan and his mom. I was so excited that I wasn't thinking, and the first thing I said was that I was going home next week. Here was this man, who I had just met, who was in the middle of a long rehab stay at the hospital and I was bragging to him about leaving. He didn't let it slide, either. He had a few choice words for me, which I can't repeat. I deserved it and took what he had to dish out. He smiled and then looked out of the window to one side.

"Is it a sunny day?" Donovan asked me, squinting.

I told him that, in fact, it was warm and sunny. He said he could tell that it was bright, but that was all.

He had been rendered blind by the fire.

I did not know Donovan Williams before the fire, now I count him among my best friends. He was 33 at the time, from Westerly, Rhode Island. He is an intelligent man, creative and confident. He graduated from Providence's renowned fine arts college, Rhode Island School of Design as a graphic artist. He is a divorced father of three young children. In fact, his divorce had become final only four days before the fire, adding another hardship on top of everything else he was going through at the time. He had been going to The Station for many years, and the one night we all wished we had skipped was also the one that had brought us together.

Donovan sustained burns on over 60% of his body. The heat and chemicals of the fire damaged the optical nerve of both eyes, rendering him virtually blind. Yet despite all this, the night of the fire he managed to walk out of the burning building under his own power and to an ambulance. He was taken to Rhode Island Hospital before being choppered to Massachusetts General, where he was given a 30% chance of survival. He battled through multiple infections as well as a dangerous blood clot and renal failure. The severe swelling resulting from the catastrophic burns created enormous pressure on his internal organs and hindered them from functioning properly. As a result, his stomach was cut open and his intestines were temporarily placed outside his body to relieve the compression and allow his vital organs to work.

Like me, Donovan had been placed in a medically-induced coma. When I arrived at MGH we became neighbors. He was in the room right next door to mine. For a month and a half as we lay in beds separated only by one thin wall, our conscious minds somewhere far off in another plane of existence, both of our families had gotten to know each other. Since both of our families were there all day, every day, they got to know each other quite well. It started out with a simple wave and saying hello while passing by one another as they were coming and going, then meeting together in the hallway and talking. Eventually it progressed to having coffee in the cafeteria, exchanging phone numbers and getting together with one another outside the hospital.

It wasn't just our parents who bonded with each other. It was siblings, cousins, friends. Everyone. The children would play together.

They eventually came to rely on one another to help get them through what was an awful experience, a terrifying and defenseless ordeal which they thought no one else could understand. The bond they formed was so strong that there existed in each family a very real fear that one day they would show up at the hospital to find the room across the hall quiet, the bed empty, the vigil abandoned. In that sense, they became like one big extended family, visiting two sick relatives in the hospital at the same time.

Six weeks after I had been transferred to MGH, Donovan was fifty pounds lighter when we were both brought out of our comas on the same day. The transition was not an easy one for him, either. He also woke to sometimes amusing, often terrifyingly hallucinations. In some of them he was hanging out with rock legends. In others, he was being assisted by a nurse into a bed that was in his back yard. Various anti-psychotic mediations were prescribed by his doctors, but they did little to keep the hallucinatory images, or his anxiety, at bay. Blind, scared and in pain, he would sometimes beg his caregivers to put him out of his misery.

The relationship between the members of our families continued to develop after we regained full consciousness. As both of us became more aware of our surroundings, and our trachs were removed and we could communicate somewhat, we learned about each other from our families, but had yet to meet. I could, however, clearly hear Donovan next door. Every night, all night, he was very vocal as he called for his nurses. I could also hear some of the nurses nearby respond, "Oh! There goes Donovan again," or "It's your turn to see what he wants this time."

He wasn't complaining or being difficult so much as this was his personality, something I would find out for myself later as I got to know him. He just wanted some company, someone to talk to, tell a joke to. He has a naturally dynamic and engaging personality, so human contact was something he was used to in whatever form it took. In the situation he was in, it was also something he needed. And he made sure he got it, that's for sure.

You might think that Donovan would be too physically drained, overly medicated or depressed to be so boisterous. Having just awakened from a prolonged coma, sleep was the last thing he would have wanted to do. I could relate to that. It was something we dealt with in our own way. Donovan harassed the nursing staff, I left my television on. The only thing that seemed to be on late at night was the show, *COPS*. I never really watched it. I just wanted to have some kind of distraction. The volume was high, especially for 2 a.m., and the night nurses were always telling me to turn it off and get to sleep.

At the time, Donovan and I were both still learning about the extent of our injuries, as well as the prognosis and limitations that were their consequences.

Truth be told, if anyone had a right to complain it would have been Donovan. But he never did. He never felt sorry for himself. He didn't succumb to anger or pity. He sustained horrific fifth degree burns to more than half of his body.

Most people have never heard of fifth degree burns. The most common system of classifying burns categorizes them as first-, second-, or third-degree. Sometimes this is extended to include burns up to a sixth degree, with these higher classifications being so severe that they are typically used to categorize post-mortem burns.

A newer classification describes burn injuries as "Superficial Thickness," "Partial Thickness," or "Full Thickness." Superficial often relates to typical sunburn, while partial thickness involves extensive damage to the upper layers of skin, and full-thickness indicates that the burn has gone through the skin and into the underlying layers of tissue.

Regardless of what they are called, Donovan's burns were extremely serious and usually fatal. The deepest burns extended to the muscle tissue, which was exposed and partially charred in places. The worst areas were on his backside, legs and buttocks. Nerve damage to his limbs left his fingers and toes in a permanent clawed position. On top of this, having lost his sight, his career as a graphic artist, something he truly loved, almost certainly had been lost as well.

Although Donovan's burn injuries were both life-threatening and life-altering, his personality remained unchanged. He was as witty, upbeat and engaging as he had been before the fire. During the later stages of my recovery, when we were both home, he pretty much served as my personal role model. I had never been through anything like this before, but seeing the way Donovan handled the traumas we both faced made it easier for me to continue to be myself, and not change my outlook on life.

Donovan has the most amazing attitude in which he is able to accept what he cannot change while at the same time letting everyone know explicitly, *this is who I am, so get used to it.* He makes no apology for his love of heavy metal music. He would dress the same way after his recovery as he did before the fire, wearing his rock T-shirts, zip-up hoodie sweatshirts, long hair, the mullet in the back. He had tattoos on his arms which had been burnt off, and if it were possible he would have gotten new ones to replace them even though much of his skin has been permanently marked by what happened on February 20, 2003.

On the weekends, I knew he would be visited by his children, whose faces he could make out only dimly. When his ex-wife told him how well Zach, his oldest son was doing in Little League Baseball, it tore him up. He asked her to videotape some of the games so that he might one day view them if some of his vision returned.

Eventually, he would gain about 30% of his vision back in his left eye, only enough to see shadowy shapes and movement, but it gave him an incredible lift.

I think it was for all these reasons that I admired Donovan. I think anyone would.

I know that our paths crossed as a result of a tragedy, but I count myself very lucky to have Donovan in my life. No matter what else the future has in store for me, we will always be friends.

CHAPTER 10   COMING HOME

The day I left Spaulding was also the day that I looked at myself in the mirror for the first time since the fire. Up until that point, only the people at the hospital would see me, so it didn't care what I looked like. However, now that I was moving on, I realized that I had reached a point where I *needed* to look in order to continue my rehab and get through it successfully.

My therapist was with me as I was getting ready to go home. An aid helped me shower, and when we finished we went back to my room, where my therapist asked me what I wanted to do. I knew what she meant. She had been telling me for some time to look in the mirror. Now that I was going home, she thought it was time for me to confront my injuries. I knew she was right and hesitantly agreed.

"It's not as bad as you think," she kept insisting.

I had been envisioning something like Freddy Krueger from *A Nightmare on Elm Street*. She brought in a full length mirror and had me partially undress. My heart was pounding as I stepped in front of it and slowly lifted my head to meet my own gaze. What I saw caused me to let out a deep sigh of relief. I was so elated I wanted to cry. Kristen was telling me the truth. It wasn't as bad as I imagined it. It wasn't good, don't get me wrong, but it had also been only four months since the fire, so it could have been a lot worse.

One side of my face was pink and mottled with scar tissue. I knew I had lost my ear, so I was prepared for that. I saw the places on my back that had been burnt for the first time. Seeing myself without hair, and knowing that it would probably never grow back, was more difficult.

Now, with my stay at Spaulding Hospital drawing to a close, I could say with absolute certainty that there was no better facility in existence for me to begin the enormous physical and emotional healing that I needed to undergo.

I learned so much during my time at Spaulding; about courage, dedication, about inner strength and the power of never giving up. I also learned that I was just one of the thousands of patients that Spaulding helps every year with their own unique and often complex recoveries. Each and every day patients confronting long odds and high hurdles make enormous strides toward returning to functional lives at Spaulding's main campus in Boston or at one of their six outpatient centers throughout eastern Massachusetts.

I didn't know how special Spaulding was until I arrived there myself, or more accurately, it wasn't until I was leaving the hospital that I realized its true value. Spaulding's reputation as one of the country's preeminent rehabilitation hospitals, however, is no secret. Patients recovering from an array of injuries, including brain surgery, spinal cord injuries, strokes, joint replacements, chronic pain and sports injuries, have access to an unbeatable spectrum of healthcare professionals, including physicians from thirty specialties and rehabilitative disciplines.

Spaulding is a place where the finest minds in rehabilitative health care come to learn and to share what they've discovered. They conduct cutting-edge scientific research in rehabilitation with the goal of improving the quality of life for their patients. And as part of Harvard Medical School's Physical Medicine and Rehabilitation Residency Program, Spaulding provides training and internship opportunities to more than 400 students per year in physician medical specialties, nursing, speech pathology, physical therapy, occupational therapy, medical social services and other clinical disciplines.

While my complete recovery was many days off, it is because of the expert care I received at Spaulding that I knew I could endure the pain and challenges that still lie ahead and continue to make steady progress.

My every moment at Spaulding was infused with abundant hope and extraordinary care. Never did I feel that I was alone in my struggle to recover and regain mobility. These individuals, with whom I laughed and cried on a daily basis the previous six weeks, never for one second let me believe that my recovery was impossible. They transformed my heart and soul and made my body strong again. They understood my fears, felt my pain and shared my joy at the most seemingly minor accomplishment. The day I was able to brush my teeth on my own, they made me feel like I had scaled a mountain. After only six weeks at Spaulding, I could see a light shining at the end of a long, dark tunnel.

The day I left the facility turned out to be a very difficult day for me. I became very emotional. This caught me a little by surprise. I thought that when the time finally came I wouldn't be able to get out of there fast enough and never look back. Just the opposite was true, however.

I was more than happy to be going home, but a harrowing despair came over me when I thought about all the people that I had gotten to know at the hospital and would never see again. I was going to miss them and the interactions I had with everyone there, the patients as well as the staff. I even felt guilty because I was the first Station Fire survivor to be discharged from the hospital, while Donovan Williams and others were stuck there. I felt like I was abandoning them and all the people who had cared for me, including the doctors and therapists who helped me walk again. They had all gained an immediate and permanent place in my heart.

They even had a big party for me, sending me off with much fanfare. Many of the hospital staff, doctors and nurses gathered in the lobby and cheered as I was leaving. Some were crying. It was overwhelming, and a little embarrassing. I did everything I could to keep a brave face and not collapse in a heap in front of them. If I had fallen down, I probably wouldn't have been able to get back up. Now that would be embarrassing. Not only that, but it might change the hospital's assessment and they might not let me go home. Somehow, I managed to stay on my feet.

As I was walking out the doors of Spaulding for the last time, one of my doctors told me that I would be fine and not to feel bad, that I would be a part of them forever, and to not even think that I would never see them again.

It made me feel good to hear that. And they never did abandon me. The care continued after I left. The staff at Spaulding had already made arrangements to have a therapist visit me every day while I was home.

So after six weeks of grueling therapy I was discharged from Spaulding Rehabilitation Hospital. It was Friday the13th, of all days, when I went home for the first time since the fire, exactly 113 days before.

I'll never forget that ride home from the hospital with my mom and step dad. I had been away nearly four months, but it seemed as if I hadn't been home in years. Spring was giving way to summer and everything was so beautiful. The last time I'd seen anything outside of a hospital room window it was cold and there was snow on the ground. Now, everything was green, pure, alive. My senses were overpowered with the beauty of nature. The trees full of leafs. The sounds of birds. The smell of blooming flowers. I could practically taste the drifting pollen in the air.

As soon as we pulled into the driveway I began to cry as hard as I ever cried in my life. I couldn't help it. It just felt so good to be home, and seeing the house that was so familiar to me. The way the weeds grew in one corner of the garden, escaping the reach of the lawnmower blades. The new section of the fence that had been repaired two summers ago and still needed to be painted. All the mundane things that you take for granted because you see them all the time, suddenly it was as if I was seeing them all for the first time. I noticed that replacement windows had been installed, and that made the old house look new again.

My boys were at school, which was on alert. Everyone knew I was coming soon, but they didn't know exactly when it would be. Alex and Nicholas didn't even know. I wanted to surprise them, so after my step dad dropped us off he drove to the school to pick them up. My mother called the principal to got permission to have Alex and Nicholas dismissed for the rest of the day. They came running into the house and we were all crying and laughing at the same time.

From the moment I awakened into my new life as a post Station Fire survivor, I've gotten so much support and felt so much affection from family, friends and people I'd never met, but by far the best feeling in the world was to be loved by such two wonderful sons. It was something to cherish.

I immediately seemed to fall right back in step with my previous, everyday life. My oldest son had a Little League baseball game that first night and I went to see him play like I had done so many times before, except this time I was all bandaged up. His team ended up winning the championship and it was something else to celebrate.

Later, when we got home, we were all kind of quiet. It had been an emotionally exhausting day and we were all so happy to be together again, there was nothing that anyone could have said that would have made it any more special. But quiet moments were also dangerous, and despite the positive start to my homecoming the reality of just how much my life had changed could not be overlooked. This was a time of emotional adjustment for me that was extraordinarily difficult on occasion. Despite how far I had come, the psychological impact of starting my life over again at my age, with two growing boys, was overwhelming. I couldn't help thinking, *Now what? What am I going to do? How am I going to support my family? What was going to become of my sons if I couldn't provide for them?* I asked God why He had me survive. For what? I felt useless. Good-for-nothing.

In the beginning, I found that I couldn't get comfortable in my own house. I did not feel like myself. I didn't want to be a burden, or have my family have to take care of me. I thought, maybe I should have stayed in the hospital. My parents were older. My children are too young. I should be taking care of them.

It was also a time when Fred's death really started to hit me.

When I was alone, it was the worst. There were no doctors around. No nurses. No therapists. When I finally had a moment to really think I would dwell on Fred's death, the life together that we had lost and what might have been. Fred and I had been talking about marriage. We had been looking at houses. All that was gone now.

The doctors had told me that I *was* a different person now, and that it would be easier for me if I just forgot about the person that I had been. But I couldn't do that. That was the person who had been in love with Fred. I couldn't just not love him anymore.

I realized that these aspects of my life had changed forever, but I did not want to let go of the past. This way of thinking has been a salvation for me during my stay at the hospital, but it could also become a hindrance to me now that I was home.

In my mind, I couldn't help thinking how Fred might have suffered at the end of his life. How he had pushed me closer to the door ahead of him to try to get me away from the flames. How that might have helped save my life and cost him his own. I thought about how my physical impairment would never allow me to meet another man, let alone get married. I cried for all of these things, and I cried a lot.

I went through all the emotions. For a while I was very angry. I directed it toward the wrong people, especially the nurses. I associated them with the situation I was in, my pain, my disfigurement, my guilt, even though they were trying to help me.

There was always someone in the house, and I just wanted to be left alone. I didn't want to be touched. I didn't want to talk to anyone. I couldn't get away from them fast enough. I wanted to just lock myself in my room and escape it all. I didn't think I had any reason to come out again.

I was very self-conscious about my appearance, and I imagine I always will be to a certain degree. I would panic when I had to meet people for the first time. I didn't want anyone, including nurses and therapists, to look at me. It was difficult enough for me to look at myself. I didn't want to make other people feel uncomfortable. Despite the parts of me that had been lost in the fire, I suppose my vanity was still intact.

One example of this was when the hospital where I worked wanted to have a secondary insurance company evaluate me. I flat out refused to allow another set of eyes pore over my body. I told them that they could keep their damn insurance money, I wouldn't submit to another physical exam. If all the burn surgeons I've seen already weren't enough for them, then I didn't want their money. I don't need it. It wasn't worth the humiliation. They eventually got back in touch with me and told me that I didn't need to go through a physical, after all.

I knew that this temperament was not a healthy one, and that it would not do me any good, only hurt me. But I couldn't help it. I did that for a long time. But this wasn't me, and it was tearing me apart inside.

I realized that the people I was shunning, my community, my neighbors, my friends, were the same people who had done so much for me and my children while I was away. This was the beginning of another awakening of sorts for me. I could never repay these people for what they did. I'll never even know all the things they did. The best thing I could do was get well and take care of my family. That may have been easier said than done, but that's what I decided to do. Try to do, anyway.

I also realized that I had no choice but to let the people who loved me help me. There were many everyday tasks that I just could not perform for myself. Things such as tying my shoes and shaving my legs. I could not articulate my hands to wash myself. My mother would help me shower, but that eventually became too much for her and a home health aide came in to assist me. It was even more of a humbling experience to have a strange person do this for me, but I needed the help.

I knew I had my work cut out for me. It was the pretty much the same routine as in the hospital. Nurses or home health care aids would come in twice a day to change my dressings. Soon, my hands were unwrapped, but my head was not.

The Oxycodone they prescribed for me was enough to keep most of pain and discomfort at bay, and it was especially welcome as even more grafts were performed. However, I remember being shocked by the list of painkillers I had been taking during my hospitalization. The level of medications was so high, in fact, that I had to be put on methadone, which I had been taking in weaning doses right up until the day I left Spaulding. Before I came home I was adamant about being off methadone because I did not want to have that stuff around the house. I had two young sons so I made sure I had completely weaned myself off any of the hard addictive narcotics I had been taking, and I was sent me home only with Oxycodone.

I had physical and occupational therapy every morning. I was progressing nicely, but so slowly. My recovery couldn't happen fast enough.

CHAPTER 11   GREAT WHITE WHALE

The criminal aspect of this regional tragedy and personal nightmare was inching forward at a snail's pace. While blame for the fire continued to spread like an oil spill, no arrests had been made and nobody had been indicted. Meanwhile, my lawyers set a target file date for filing their civil complaint the following summer. Their list of defendants had grown to fifty-eight, both individuals, such as the Derderian brothers, Daniel Biechele and Jack Russell of Great White, as well as corporations with substantially deeper pockets. These included Anheuser-Busch, Clear Channel Broadcasting and the manufacturers, distributors and sellers of the foam used to soundproof the nightclub.

These comprehensive legal actions, however, were not being taken solely for my benefit and protection. My lawyer, Mark S. Mandell, was also the co-chair of a Plaintiff's Steering Committee that involved eight other law firms. They were all working together to file a *unified complaint* on behalf of over 226 plaintiffs, including families of ninety of the victims and 176 of the injured survivors. The case was the largest of nine other lawsuits that had been brought on behalf of the families and survivors, and I can say with no uncertainty that it was not being taken solely for financial gain. There was a genuine need to, if not right a grave wrong, then to ease some of the suffering and burden that the survivors of The Station Fire would have to bear for the rest of their lives.

On June 30, Jeffrey Derderian officially resigned as a news reporter with Channel 12. He realized he could no longer do that very public job, and hadn't worked on any stories since the fire. For many people, to see him on television again would only serve as another painful and unnecessary reminder of the lost and ruined lives for which he had been largely responsible. I know I wouldn't have watched that news station again if there was a chance of seeing his face on their newscast. I'm sure I wouldn't have been the only one. WPRI-TV would have been more than aware of the potential for such a boycott, as would Clear Channel, the station's parent company, both of whom were being sued as part of the civil lawsuit.

Jeffrey Derderian had once filed a report on a story about the hazards of mattress fires. He had been working for a Boston TV station at the time, and referred to the polyurethane foam, common in many mattresses, as 'solid gasoline.' Well, he may as well have tacked gasoline soaked rags to the walls. It was basically the same material that he had cocooned around the interior of The Station nightclub at his authorization, and it enveloped every patron who had ever entered the establishment under his and his brother's ownership. Yet somehow the Derderians, as well as West Warwick fire safety inspectors, were blissfully unaware of these facts prior to February 20, 2003.

On July 7, Governor Carcieri signed "The Comprehensive Fire Safety Act of 2003," which completely overhauled the state's fire safety codes. Some of those codes had been in desperate need of revision for decades, having aged to the point of becoming completely obsolete and obviously dangerous. Unfortunately, it took a catastrophe of this scale to change them. I can't say I'm happy to have played a part in this long-overdue revision of Rhode Island's fire safety codes, unknowingly sacrificing my health and Fred's life, but kudos to the governor and our lawmakers for working so hard to have these changes made so quickly. No one could change the past or what had happened at The Station, but at least the future could be altered so that another fire of this magnitude might be averted.

In August, Jack Russell's name surfaced again when he provided the media with a public comment. As if taunting the families and survivors, he vowed to mark the half year anniversary of the fire with a private vigil. He also told reporters that he would continue to play benefit concerts to raise money for The Station Family Fund (TSFF). Over the last month, Russell had played nine shows and claimed to have raised $21,622 for TSFF. There were fifteen more shows scheduled through the end of September, and he said that helping to raise money for survivors and victim's families was the reason he gets up in the morning. No shows in New England had been scheduled, and when asked about a possible concert in Rhode Island, Russell said he would play there if it was appropriate, and that he didn't want to upset anyone. He knew he would never be completely welcomed here, but he said he would be willing to play here so that he could raise more money for the Fund.

Speaking on behalf of the survivors, I can say with certainty that many of us felt that the next time Russell and Great White came back to the area it would be too soon. If he wasn't going to be formally charged and listed on a bill of indictment, we didn't want to hear his name again. Everyone wished he would just go away forever.

In the same interview, he referred to the fire as an "American Tragedy," not just a "Rock 'n Roll Tragedy," and he called on individuals to donate. He also challenged other bands to take up the cause, especially mega bands like KISS, who could generate more proceeds to the Fund from one concert than Great White could over the course of a year.

Russell also claimed that the support of his fans during this difficult time had changed his life. He seemed to be saying that fame and money comes and goes, but the genuine feelings of people who love and understand you is what matters most.

All very touching and heartfelt, and I'm not going to challenge him on those remarks. I couldn't tell you what was actually going on in his mind, because he and God are the only ones who know that. I can tell you this, when he said that he was playing all those concerts and donating the proceeds to The Station Family Fund, it was not true. Every dime that has come in since the inception of TSFF has been meticulously accounted for, and as of the printing of this book Jack Russell and Great White have contributed nothing to it. The only person who benefited from those concerts was Jack Russell. In fact, it reached a point where Russell was asked to put up or shut up. Victoria Potvin, the president of The Station Family Fund at the time, informed Great White's front man in no uncertain terms to cease and desist from going around and promoting his concerts as a benefit to the Fund if he was not going to follow through with the donations.

Regardless of how much money, real or imagined, Russell contributed to the Fund, there was no love lost between him and many of the survivors, especially with me. His accountability for that fire was *very* real, yet this plain truth was seemingly, inconceivably, being dismissed by both himself and state prosecutors. So far, there had been absolutely no talk that Jack Russell was being looked at with any serious consideration for criminal indictment by the Rhode Island Attorney General. It just wasn't happening, but we were all still holding out hope that in the end he was going to be named as one of the defendants when the indictments were handed down in the next couple of months.

People can debate this issue with me forever, but I will never compromise my belief that Jack Russell had authorized the use of those pyrotechnics and that he was the one and only person who could have seen to it that the gerbs never left the safety of their packing cases that night.

Personally, I have nothing against Jack Russell. I don't know the man. But I do know for a fact that he contributed extensively to the fire that killed Fred and ninety-nine other people.

It never reached the point of obsession, but in the end Jack Russell may have become a white whale of sorts for many of us. The difference being that Herman Melville's Captain Ahab was only chasing *one* elusive beast. The Station Fire was not caused by the negligence and carelessness of just one person, or by the professional dereliction of a state inspection board. It may be much simpler to blame a cow for starting the Great Chicago Fire, but it took many hands and blind eyes to set into motion the disaster at the nightclub in West Warwick.

It's no great mystery to anyone who knows Jack Russell that he had an affinity for pyrotechnics. He insisted on having them at every venue Great White played. He wanted to have them at The Station, and didn't exercise an ounce of common sense when he saw how small the facility was, how low the ceilings were or how many people were packed inside. He didn't think the sparks would touch off a fire. And that's exactly right, *he didn't think*. He didn't think that if a fire broke out, people were going to die. Right, again. *He didn't think*. It's the very definition of gross criminal negligence. If Daniel Biechele had refused to trigger the pyrotechnics that night, someone else would have. Jack Russell would have seen to that. He probably would have triggered them himself if he couldn't get anyone else to do it.

It was around this time that Larry King extended an invitation to Station Fire survivors, asking them to appear on a future segment of his CNN talk show. I had originally planned to attend with several survivors, including Donovan Williams, who was scheduled to be released from the hospital soon. However, before we left for California we learned that Russell's lawyer and a former member of Great White were going to be there as well. I was immediately advised by my lawyer not to get on the plane. It was a wise decision. I don't know what I would have said, or done, if I found myself in the presence of someone who represented Jack Russell. It would not have been good for anyone, so I stayed home.

It seemed as if I was gaining more and more independence as the weeks went by, but it may have been only wishful thinking on my part. I still needed a lot of assistance from my family, and they continued to be there for me.

Besides the home visitations by my therapists, I had to be driven to Boston at least twice a week to see my doctors for evaluation or to undergo further surgical procedures. Even at this stage of my recovery, it took a concerted effort by my family to coordinate the driving and the sitting of my boys. This would continue for several years I was told, though the visits would become less frequent, curtailing to one day per week, then every other week and eventually seldom to never.

I was determined, however, to be driving myself long before then. In fact, I had aspirations of being behind the wheel by October. Nobody believed I could do it, and my doctors probably thought it was just more self-deception, but I wouldn't have said it if I didn't intend to follow through with it.

August 16, 2003

On February 20, 2003 my life changed forever. It is now six months later and I still cannot understand any of this. My boyfriend Alfred Crisostomi died in this nightmare that doesn't seem to end. I miss him more as each day passes and sometimes don't want to go on. Then I remind myself of how lucky I am to be able to be here with my two wonderful children Alexander and Nicholas along with the rest of my family who kept vigil over me while I was at Shriners Hospital for 5 weeks, Massachusetts General Hospital and then Spaulding Rehab. I cannot believe that this is me because my appearance has changed so

much. At this point I have had at least 10 surgeries with more to come (maybe for the rest of my life). My arms and back are severely burned I lost my left ear and will never have my own hair again. Pretty sad for someone who is only 35-years old. I will look like this forever and that will allow me to never forget this mess. I have so much anger for the Derderian brothers, the bouncer who would not let us out the door because it was club policy not to open the door except for anyone but the band (well, what made their life more important than mine?) I cry every day for all that I have lost and for what I will never have or be able to do again. Like not being with the Fred and being able to hug and kiss him every day (he was going to be my husband) you have no idea, and never will, of the loss I feel for him and all of the independence you took away from me. I can no longer work at a job I've had for 19 years. I have to watch every dime I spend because of having to live on social security for the rest of my life at the age of 35 that's pretty sad how will I ever be able to help my two children go to college or help with their future like a parent should. You have taken so much from me and I will bet that neither of you will ever have to worry about money or how you are going to send your children to school. Your stupidity and greed has cost 300 people so much heartache and grief you will never understand the depth of this pain until the day the you are sentenced to spending your days in hell where you will feel the pain of fire and the smell of burning for me your time will not come soon enough I hope I get the chance to live long enough to witness that day (hopefully the lung damage I was left with won't get me first). I can only hope that the justice system will take into consideration the life sentence you have given to 300 people when your times comes to pay for what you have done.
This is not the end of my story it's just the beginning of what will be a lifetime of pain and suffering.

CHAPTER 12   FRIENDS IN FIRE

In August, when Donovan Williams was discharged from Spaulding, I got the news from my family, who remained in contact with members of his family. After a lengthy rehabilitation, he was placed in the care of a nursing home in Westerly, RI.

It was during this time that Donovan reached out to me and we began to communicate on a regular basis. Whenever he needed someone to talk to he would call me and we'd stay on the phone for hours. Our conversations were about everything except the fire. We would discuss our children, divorce and music. Slowly, we got to know each other and became close. We came to rely on one another for support and friendship.

It was a very difficult time for Donovan. He remained virtually blind. Although he would slowly get back about 25% of his vision, doctors have said that it will not improve any further. His excruciating rehab would last for many, many months. He was participating in physical therapy three times a week. Both of his hands had been severely burnt, and while surgery managed to save them from amputation, the numerous grafts have crippled them and rendered them useless. He was working hard at regaining the strength in his right hand, which was similar to that of a seven-year old. His left hand is not much better off, having lost the tip of the thumb.

He was unable to work. He was uninsured. The Social Security benefits he began receiving were not enough to cover his living expenses. The Station Family Fund stepped in and paid his mortgage for several months, as well as some of the cost for running his air conditioner, which he needed to have on all the time because he was extremely sensitive to heat. His temporary disability insurance was about to run out, while the total cost of his medical care reached the $5 million mark. In spite of all this, Donovan always had a smile on his face.

He soon moved out of the nursing facility and into the home of his married sister, who lived nearby with her three grown daughters. Like me, he was fortunate to have a great family who was there for him. This was the period when we probably got to know each other best. It didn't take him long to start dating again. He was a bachelor again, and he didn't let his injuries keep him from moving on with his life.

I had communicated with other survivors, as well, though mostly through e-mails because I had been reluctant to go out in public. It was scary for me. I didn't know any of these people and I didn't think we had anything in common besides the fire, so for a long time I kept a physical distance. Donovan was one of the few people I spoke with, so our friendship developed first.

In contrast to Donovan, I've always been much less comfortable with my injuries and my appearance. For the longest time I would never even consider meeting anyone. I *didn't want to* meet anyone. Fred was so much a part of my every thought, how would I have been able to give my heart to anyone? Each time Donovan had a date, and it was often, he would call me afterward to tell how it had gone. He tried to encourage me to get back out on the dating scene, as well, but every time I would tell him that nobody would take me out the way I looked. He told me I was crazy. Just making excuses. To sell my point, I would describe what I looked like, but he wouldn't buy it.

It may have helped that he could not see the extent of his injuries, despite having full knowledge of them. It might be difficult for most people to conceptualize something they have never seen before, but I wouldn't put anything past Donovan. I remember one time, it was a hot, humid afternoon, and he nonchalantly peeled his shirt off and asked me how his back looked. It was one deep, massive scar. It had been extensively grafted, and the doctors had done a fantastic job, but Donovan was not the least bit self-conscious.

I'll never forget the first time that I went out in a public setting. It was during a gathering that Donovan and I had been planned with other survivors. We had established our own little support group, and began meeting at one another's house. This time, however, we made reservations at a restaurant. It was a big step for many of us, including me. There were about fifteen of us that night. We had the most incredible time. Donovan's sense of humor was in some kind of hyper drive that night. You would never have known how much he was suffering. He had everyone laughing, not only at our table but people at the tables around us.

There were all enjoying the Donovan Show. It was great for all of us to be around each other, Donovan in particular.

As I got to know some of the other survivors, I found that we genuinely liked one another and shared, among other things, a love of music. As we began going out together more often, including taking in some rock concerts, we would refer to ourselves as "The Misfits." This was not only because we looked different, we also felt different. Around each other, however, we found that we could embrace who we were. In each other's company, we were suddenly okay with it, with everything. And that was special. I know I felt comfortable. We could be ourselves, and didn't care what other people thought. There were a few places where we would meet, certain clubs that played the kind of music we liked. We had our own corner of the bar where we would gather, so that anyone who showed up could easily find us. We will still do this even today occasionally, though attendance and frequency has been dropping off steadily as everyone has gotten on with their own lives. That is to say, our lives have taken us to better places, and we don't depend on each other the way we once did. That said, it is an unspoken truth that we will always be there for anyone in a time of need. Even if we do not see someone for several years, if they were to have a problem at anytime we would be there for them one hundred percent.

Linda Fisher is someone I had known before the fire. She is a wonderful friend. Linda and a bartender named Julie were the only two people, besides Fred, who I had known at The Station the night of the fire. I remember asking about them soon after I came out of my coma. I wanted to know what happened to them, and I was relieved to find out that Linda had survived, though she was badly burned, and that Julie was fortunate to have made it out of the club through the kitchen door completely unharmed. Still, Julie has experienced as much emotional trauma as any survivor as a direct result of her good fortune and having to cope with a profound sense of guilt. Unfortunately, this is something that survivors sometimes go through, and can lead to any number of health problems, addictive behavior and even suicide. Tragically, there have been several survivors of The Station Fire that wound up taking their own lives in the months following the disaster. There have also been incidences of rescue workers and firefighters attempting or committing suicide because of their experiences that

February night. These poor souls, however, are not counted among the fire fatalities, which will forever stand at one hundred.

Julie has told me many times that she does not understand why she hadn't been burned while so many others, including myself, had suffered so much. *You didn't deserve it,* she would tell me. *You didn't deserve to lose Fred.*

What she also couldn't understand was that I was grateful that she had not been hurt. Nobody deserved to be injured or killed. But it happened, and despite what I lost, I feel blessed in so many ways for all that I still have.

When channeled in a positive way, I've seen how such guilt can be put to good use and help a lot of people. Victoria Potvin, who had also escaped The Station unharmed, joined our misfits group and was responsible for starting The Station Family Fund, a charity that raised money to help survivors and their families not only with medical bills but with the daily necessities that some could no longer provide for their families or themselves.

I first met Vicki at the six-month anniversary of the fire, when many of us were gathered for a memorial service at the site in West Warwick. I knew who she was, what she was doing with The Station Family Fund, and I approached her and told her that she was beautiful, that I was glad she had made it out safely. She just looked at me and began crying. She told me she couldn't understand how I could say that, particularly considering the way I looked at the time, with my head wrapped in gauze and my body wizened and stiff from burns and surgery. I explained that it was wonderful that so many people had escaped unscathed. I only wish it had been more.

The new friendships I formed during this time were not limited to survivors. By chance, Donovan and I had the same Blue Cross case worker. Her name is Stephanie Niewola, and she handled all the medical billing and claims that needed to be filed on our behalf. Talk about a paper chase. We would have been lost without her, for sure. But she was great, and eventually we both began to build up such a good rapport with her that she began making personal calls to us, which had nothing to do with Blue Cross. She didn't know that Donovan and I were close and we didn't know she was handling both of us. When we found out we became like The Three Musketeers. She looked out for us, making sure we had everything we needed from our doctors and our insurance, everything. She is also a nurse. She was our biggest protector. She soon became part of our crew when we all went out together. She may not have had the scars that we did, but she was one of us and she's one of my best friends now.

On a sad note, on August 20, Lisa Marie Scott died at home after an accidental fall. Exactly six months after she had been rescued from the fire, Lisa fell down a flight of stairs and suffered massive trauma to her head from which she could not recover.

After having battled great odds to survive the fire, it's almost inconceivable that she would lose her life this way. Lisa went from becoming a survivor to victim of the fire, but she would never be listed as a casualty because the burn injuries she suffered did not lead directly to the loss of her life.

Lisa left behind a husband and three children. She was 33.

August 23, 2003

Thank you Freddy for all you gave me and my children in the 10 months we were together. I hope that someday we will be together again when my time on earth is done. I wish every day and pray every day that you are ok. I miss you more as each day passes. I miss everything we did together and mourn what could have been a great life for both of us. You gave me so many happy and loving times that I will cherish for all the rest of my days. I miss our intimate time together when we could be ourselves and explore new things together. You brought something out in me that I didn't know existed thank you for that and so much more. My children miss you so very much you would have made a great father to them and they will always love you. Freddy, there are so many things I need to talk to you about. I need you here with me so I could have someone to go through this with. I don't look the same but I have to believe that you would not have cared about that and I need to believe that we would have overcome this mess together and I believe that this would have brought us even closer together than we already were. You gave me a new life and hope for a future. Someday, if I ever have grand-children they will know about you and how happy you made me and the boys. I am angry at so many people for taking you away from me, the boys and your family. When you left this earth I did not know for 10 weeks because of the condition I was in and hearing that you were no longer with me I felt like my whole world died with you. At first, it was so hard to comprehend that you died and I lived through this nightmare with some pretty serious injuries. The doctor called it survivor guilt. The feeling was so strong I wished God would take me so you would not have to be alone. Later I came to understand that I was kept alive and God must have a reason and a new plan for me. Maybe it's just to raise my children who need me so much. I need to believe that you're not mad at me for living and will be my angel to help guide me through what is going to be many years of hell. August 20th 2003 was six months since that awful night and I went to the Station to be with you I felt some peace being there because it's where your spirit is and I so badly need to feel you around me. I love you with all my heart and soul for all eternity. Thank you for loving me and giving me 10 months of happiness and most of all your love. Until you came along my life was on hold and you opened so many doors and feelings I had never experienced. I will remember our time together with so much love and also with longing for what could have been and what will never be. You are my life, my love, my heart forever. Please always be there for me when I need someone to talk to. I will call upon you and I will pray for you always. I will be forever yours, Freddy Crisostomi.

CHAPTER 13   GETTING A SECOND CHANCE

From the very beginning of my therapy, my knees were a real source of concern. Walking is always a priority. It represents independence and freedom more than any other physical activity. My doctors had already told me that I would never have full use of my legs, and that I would not be able to drive again.

To this day, I don't know if the doctors kept telling me that I couldn't do certain things because they wanted to motivate me, but that's what happened. I was not going to accept any of the limitations that were being placed on my recovery. I was determined to prove them wrong and get back the use of my legs, at least enough to be able to drive a car. My physical therapist was just as determined. We worked hard to improve my limited range of motion. I did stretching and strengthening exercises on my own, as well, and by late August, I had more mobility than anyone anticipated. I used my success as a bargaining chip to negotiate a request for outpatient therapy. I had been stuck in the house for two and a half months and I wanted to get out, be with other people. I have to admit, I had an ulterior motive. I wanted to drive and I thought this move would expedite my progress and put me in a better position to take that next step.

The change of venue was approved by my doctors and I felt more than a little satisfaction. Because they didn't know what I was doing, it was a victory or sorts for me. Maybe it was a game I was playing, but I wanted to think I was pulling something over on them. I just wanted to have more control over my own life and body, and becoming an outpatient at Kent County Rehabilitation Center in East Greenwich for some reason gave me back some measure of independence.

Carrie was my physical therapist. Jen, my occupational therapist. They were fantastic. I loved them both. They were personal *and* professional and pushed me to where I needed to go.

Freddy, on 8/24/03 I went to a Tribute Fest to Rock music. I went for you and me because I know this is something you would have taken me to. I

*wish you were with me. You would have loved all
the bands. Human Clay is back together. Debbie,
Jimmy, Lori B, Alex and RJ came with me. Your
brother Sean was there with Jay and Jessie he
reminds me so much of you it hurts but at the
same time I feel like I am with you. At some point
when I am healed I am going to get a tattoo with a
heart and your name in it so I will never forget
what we had. I love you madly and promise never
to forget all of the good times.*

On August 27, 2003, an angel came to St. Ann Cemetery in Cranston, Rhode Island. The angel did not come from heaven, but from Carrara, Italy. The somber wooden cross representing The Station Fire victims at the cemetery's temporary memorial was about to be replaced with a more permanent and beautiful tribute. The sculpted angel was to be part of an envisioned Wall of Remembrance, which was being constructed around this magnificent centerpiece. The Eternal Angel, as it is called, was commissioned by a local monument maker, Anthony Sciolto, who donated the statue to be used as a lasting memorial to The Station Fire victims. Sciolto had originally commissioned the sculpture to sell as part of his regular business, but after the fire he knew it belonged in only one place.

The Roman Catholic Diocese of Providence, which owns the cemetery and donated the surrounding memorial and burial plots, wanted to be sure the memorial was fitting and lasting.

"We want to put something up that people will never forget," said Rev. Anthony Verdelotti, the Saint Ann Cemetery director.

The diocese also offered to donate burial plots to all Station Fire victims, regardless of their religious affiliation. Twenty of the victims are buried at Saint Ann Cemetery.

The Eternal Angel stands thirteen feet tall, with a beautiful and merciful expression on her face and a rose extended from its right hand in tribute to the deceased. It took four Italian craftsmen six months to carve the statue from native Carrara marble. The magnificent winged angel would sit atop a five-foot white granite wall, into which the names of all the fire victims would be inscribed. A central walkway would lead to the wall with the angel perched atop and flanked on each side by flat grave markers. A wrought iron fence would encompass the entire memorial site, and include four meditation benches, canopy trees, rhododendrons and weeping cherry trees.

Many local laborers and artisans would donate much of their time and considerable skills to bring the final vision of the Wall of Remembrance into existence.

It is truly a touching and magnificent tribute.

> ### *September 5, 2003*
> *Today is your birthday and I miss you terribly. I want to spend this day with you and give you whatever would make you happy. I spent some of the day with your mother and Crystal. We went to the cemetery to be with you. Your headstone is beautiful but it's so hard to look at it because I cannot imagine your beautiful body in the ground even though I know your soul is in heaven. I want you here with me, Freddy. I need you so much all I do is cry for you and everything we lost. I hope our love is strong enough and you will wait for me to come to you and then we will spend all of eternity together. I love you and please wait for me no matter how long it takes.*

In early September, I went back under the knife, this time to correct the ongoing problem that I was having with the arm. They had given physical therapy a chance, but by this point it was apparent that only surgery would correct it. Dr. Jesse Jupiter performed the operation, removing the calcium from around my elbow to free up the joint. After the surgery, Dr. Jupiter told me they were able to observe that the calcium had crushed my ulna nerve, damaging it enough so that they could not predict whether or not it would regenerate to the point where any feeling would return to my hand and allow me to use it. I also needed radiation treatments to prevent the calcium from returning.

Days later I began to get a tingly sensation in my arm, like when your arm falls asleep and it begins waking up. Only it was painful. I was thinking this was a bad sign, and I was afraid that they might have to amputate my hand. When I went in to see my neurologist, he told me that just the opposite was the case. He said it was a clear indication that the nerve was regenerating. It would be another six months, however, before I would be able to use my hand again, though not to full capacity, I was cautioned. But this was the start of something good for me. I was sure of it. After initially being told that I would probably never use my hands again, and that I would definitely never be able to drive, this was a major triumph. I wasn't going to let anyone talk me down.

Today, beyond the visible scarring, it's almost as if my hands had never been injured, though I don't have the use of my left index finger. The knuckle had been so severely burned that they removed the joint and fused the bones together, so it cannot bend. Being a lefty, it makes writing a problem, but I've learned to use my thumb and middle finger. My penmanship is still something to be desired, but my typing has actually improved. Go figure.

It's sort of ironic that with all the physical issues I faced, this index finger became the source of so many operations. In fact, the digit had been operated on so often, including numerous reconstructive surgeries and other invasive procedures to combat the perpetual problems with infection, that I had suggested to the doctors that they just remove the entire finger. To me, it just didn't seem worth all the effort, especially when you consider it does not function properly anyway. But I guess there is no sufficient argument for elective amputation, so it remains attached.

By the end of September, I was actually driving again. It was one of the happiest days I could recall, and of all my achievements so far, this one filled me with tremendous confidence and I began thinking I could do anything that I had always done before the fire.

Initially, I stayed on the side streets close to home, avoiding the highway. It felt like I did when I was sixteen and driving for the first time, excited but cautious, my head was spinning with possibilities and the promises of an independent future. It was invigorating to be able to contribute to my own life again, do something for myself and take the burden off my family. I would drive to the market, take my sons to school, and go on other errands. Everyday tasks that I used to take for granted were suddenly new. Just to be able to go to the Post Office for stamps was enjoyable.

Because of my limited range of motion, I had to have one of those blue handicap parking permits attached to my rearview mirror. My doctors and therapists documented my deficiency, but it wasn't sufficient enough to legally warrant the forfeiture of my driver's license, so I was out on the road every chance I got.

The only downside of my newfound ambitious nature were the stares I would get when I was out in the public eye. It always made me uneasy and self-conscious. Sometimes I would get very anxious, near panic, but I knew it was something I had to do. I had to get used to it if I was going to resume a normal life.

Shopping for school clothes with my kids was my first real test. My head and hands were uncovered by now, so my burns were visible to everyone. In the department stores, I noticed people would either blatantly stare or avoid looking at me altogether. I remember there was this one woman who was looking at me so long and hard that my son Alex almost went up to her to tell her to stop staring. I told him it was okay, but he was really angry. Then, because she was staring so intently at me and not paying attention to where she was going, she walked right into a wall. My son and I both laughed out loud. I have to say that after this experience I never felt as uncomfortable going out in public again. That woman did more for me than all the therapists have I ever spoken to. When I saw that woman slam into the wall so hard that she bounced off it, I thought to myself, between the two of us, she's the one who looks ridiculous.

More difficult than seeing the way strangers reacted to my burns was how some of the people closest to me responded. One of my good friends, Gayle Moore, would call me all the time, but she could not get around to see me, either at the hospital or when I was home. She just couldn't handle it, and she thought I was mad at her for that, but I wasn't. I understood. I knew her. When she finally did come to the house, about three months after I was home, it made us both feel good. She asked me, and herself out loud, *what the hell was I thinking, not visiting sooner*? Then she apologized profusely and broke down crying.

If nothing else, the tragedy made my strong relationships stronger. I also made some wonderful new friends. You do find out who your true friends are when you're in a crisis, and I found out that I had some very special people in my life. I know if may sound repetitive, but if my gratitude has reached a point of overkill, I'd prefer to go to that extreme rather than understate just how important all these people are to me. This book would not have been possible if it were not for them, because I wouldn't be alive today.

My two children were not just casual observers throughout these transitional days. They both taught me some valuable lessons on my road to recovery. One example involved my younger son, Nick. This particular incident happened at a time when I was functioning quite well, actually, and was preparing to make some brownies. Baking was something I always enjoyed. Cakes, cookies, pies, it didn't matter. But it was something I wasn't able to do for some time. I was getting back into it again this one afternoon and had asked Nick to go downstairs to bring up a mixing bowl that I needed. Well, to my utter shock, he stopped what he was doing and just looked up at me with a perturbed look on his face. Then he told me to get the bowl myself, and that I needed to learn to do things on my own.

This may seem out of context here, but he was absolutely right. I was more than capable of getting the bowl myself, I just did not want to go downstairs with my legs the way they were, so I asked him to do it. I never anticipated his reaction, and up to that point I was not at all aware of the unfair burden I had placed on him and the rest of my family and friends. Everyone had been doing so much for me, it had reached a point where maybe I was getting too dependent on others.

Well, hearing this coming from my seven-year old, I just started crying. And then he started to cry.

Later that night, he apologized for becoming upset with me, and said that he was not implying that he would never help me again. I apologized, too, and told him it was my fault for asking so much of him, not just getting bowl, but for everything that I had been asking of him. He had become so grown-up for his age and it made me sad. Our relationship had changed suddenly, and I realized that I needed to do everything I could for myself to become independent again and put myself in a better position to help my children.

I remembered, before the fire, how Nick used to sit next to me on the couch in front of the TV as we watched our favorite programs on Animal Planet. After that mixing bowl episode, it seemed we slowly started to get back into that routine again, and although it was uncomfortable for me just sitting on the couch for a long period of time, as well as a chore to stand up afterwards due to the condition of my knees, it still felt wonderful.

They say you don't know what you got until it's gone, well I was beginning to realize what I could have lost, and it made it all the more precious.

> **September 30, 2003**
> *Hi Freddy, today is a tough day I miss you so much and it's only getting worse. I saw Nancy this weekend and she gave me some of your things that I will put away in a very special box so that when I need to see you I will have something to look at. All of the small things like guitar picks and drum sticks from all of the concerts you took me to will be kept very safe because they remind me of so many good times. She gave me your USA jacket and when I wear it I feel like I can feel you so I don't ever want to stop wearing it. I need so badly to feel you near me. I feel like I am losing my connection to you, so this helps. Please don't ever forget me and always remember how happy we made each other. That is something no one can take away from us.*

It was also late that September when a major controversy was stirred up when a family member removed from the fire site in West Warwick the memorial items dedicated to Ty Longley, the Great White band member who died in the blaze. Diane Mattera, whose 29-year old daughter, Tamara Mattera-Housa, was one of the hundred victims, never tried to hide or deceive anyone that she had been responsible. Some people were appalled that she had taken two wooden crosses, a teddy bear and a guitar dedicated to the memory of the Great White drummer, along with photos of Longley's son, who was born after his death, and threw them into the woods nearby. Diane did not see what she had done as an act of vandalism.

"I just threw them into the woods," she later told the press, "because Ty does not belong there. I feel sorry for him that he died, but the only thing is, he doesn't belong there."

It was an instinctive reaction, and I'm sure many others wanted to do the same thing, or at least were secretly thinking about it. Diane is someone who doesn't hold back her feelings and emotions, and what she did had been initiated by the profound pain of her loss.

Heidi Peralta, Longley's girlfriend and mother of their infant son, Acey, was initially upset when she first learned of the incident. She later said that she empathized with Diane's anger, especially as a new mother, and held no contempt for her.

Friends and well-wishers of Longley eventually replaced the discarded wooden cross with a welded-steel cross, which they poured into a solid cement base.

They must have known, as I did, that Diane is also a very determined person.

October 18, 2003

Freddy today is my birthday and you're not here with me. I don't feel like doing anything except crying for what has been taken away from me and the future I will never have with you. Why is life so cruel? Maybe someday I will have this answer, although I am sure the answer won't be good enough for all that we have suffered. Rene has been calling me and I have met him out a couple of times for drinks but it's just not the same without you. I love and miss you more and more each day. Could you please come home to me so we can be a family? Bobby, from Backlash, called me the other night and we had a nice chat. I told him I missed hearing him play and thanked him for the many great nights he gave to you and me. I miss all of our great nights together but know that all of those great memories are mine and yours only, and at least no one can take them from us and when I feel sad and lonely I try and remember something we did together and somehow this makes me feel closer to you. Always remember how much I love you and will see you again someday.

CHAPTER 14   DAYS OF RECKONING

Around Halloween, Jimmy, my brother, snookered me into talking to someone about some of the conflicting emotional issues I was still grappling with. I have to say, in all honesty, that it wasn't done in a devious manner. My brother only wanted what was best for me, and to be happy.

I recall that my brother's car was being fixed and he had asked me if I could give him a ride to the office of a lawyer who was helping him. I, naturally, agreed. During the drive, Jimmy tried to make conversation, but I didn't feel like talking, which was not my nature at all. So we drove in silence most of the way. He didn't bring up anything about getting me back in therapy.

When we got to the building, I was going to wait in the car but he asked me come up. As James looked over and signed some documents, I sat quietly in a chair. Just as during the ride over, I didn't say much. Although things had gotten a lot better for me recently, I was having a pretty rough time and I guess it showed. It was around my birthday, I was feeling sorry for myself and I missed Fred.

It was not Jimmy, but his lawyer who suggested that I talk to a Catholic priest who had helped him through a difficult time in his life. The priest's name was Father John, from Sacred Heart Church in Pawtucket. I was never particularly religious, but I didn't want to be rude to someone who was trying to help me. And because my brother insisted I give it a try, that I had nothing to lose, I tried to keep an open mind. I set up an appointment with Father John for the following week and my brother came with me.

The priest began by explaining his ministry to me and how it worked. Basically, you talk and then pray. Every week we met and went through a different series of prayers. The first prayer involved me just introducing myself to God.

I took a deep breath and thought to myself, *okay, since He doesn't know, maybe this will refresh His memory*, then I said "I'm the burned woman whose fiancé was killed in the fires of hell by the devil at a nightclub close to where I live." Or something to that affect, anyway.

And then we prayed.

The second week, the priest acted as a liaison between me and God. Because I was still so angry, I apparently needed someone to vouch for me.

And then we prayed some more.

> **December 6, 2003**
> *Hi Freddy: I just need to talk to you so badly, but you're not here and I cannot be with you just yet so I have to write to you. It's almost Christmas and it's just not the same anymore, everything has changed in my life but the biggest loss is you. I don't think I will ever understand why you were taken away and all bad people are left here. You showed me so much about life and how to love again. Thank you for that. I need to hear your voice again and to hear you say you love me and that everything will be all right. If I could only turn back the hands of time I would never let you go. I have to stop writing for now, it hurts too much and my heart is breaking for you. I LOVE YOU WITH ALL MY HEART AND ALWAYS WILL. I am Forever Yours Freddy.*

My fifth session with Father John was supposed to be the last. By now, I should have been ready to relinquish my anger to God. In reciting a final prayer, I was basically telling God that *my anger is yours, I'm done with it. You brought this into my world for whatever reason and now I'm giving it back to you. I'm not dealing with it anymore. I'm sick and tired of being angry. I don't want to be angry anymore.*

I did everything I was supposed to do and I walked out of that church for the last time. It was December, and was snowing pretty heavily. When I got into the car afterward my brother was waiting for me. The first thing he asked was, "Well, how do you feel?"

I considered this for a moment, then looked at him and said, "I'm still pissed."

Like hypnotism, or some other form of mind control, it didn't work on me. I could not just wish for something and believe it. I needed to feel as if I had some control over my destiny, even if I did not. That's not to say that I was down on any and all attempts at redemption and acceptance. To the contrary, I was keeping my eyes and mind open for anything that might help me. I was starting to think that I was just not ready yet. Also, at that particular time, I don't think anything would have buoyed my spirits. It wasn't easy for me to stay optimistic when so much was unsettled. Emotionally speaking, it seemed like every step forward was followed by two steps backward.

Then, a few days later the Rhode Island Attorney General, Patrick Lynch, scheduled a meeting with the family members of the fire victims. It took place at the West Valley Inn in West Warwick, practically in the shadow of the fire site. The A.G.'s office was getting ready to hand down indictments, and before that information was made public Lynch wanted to pass it by the victim's families first.

Survivors were not invited to attend this dog and pony show. I had been asked because I lost Fred. The fact that I was also a survivor meant nothing to the state, from a legal standpoint. In Rhode Island, criminal charges could only be brought against suspects where the loss of life was involved. So right from the beginning, even though the A.G.'s office made this legal fact known to all, I don't think any of us truly believed that complete criminal responsibility would be discounted because there were survivors. The way this archaic state law reads, if all of the hundred victims had somehow managed to survive the fire, even with most catastrophic burns, then there would not have been any indictments at all. For many survivors, including myself, this was nothing short of disgraceful.

So we're all gathered in this big room, and as the attorney general arrives and stands before the families of the hundred people killed in the Station Fire, everyone becomes completely silent. The anticipation is tangible. Patrick Lynch tells us that the state is going forward to pursue criminal charges against Daniel Biechele, the tour manager of the band whose pyrotechnics started the fire, and the two owners of the nightclub, Michael and Jeffrey Derderian. Three people. That was it.

Now everyone sat in stunned silence. I, for one, was waiting to hear more names added to that short list. But none came.

Instead, Lynch proceeded to talk for some time, using a lot of jargon and legalese to explain why these defendants had been found and how the case would proceed. I don't know how many people were listening to anything he said after naming the three defendants, but when he was through listening to himself talk he opened this forum up to the families. For him, that turned out to be the biggest mistake for which he could *not* blame on state law. He may never admit it, but he probably regretted giving up the floor. He should have just made a hasty retreat on it while we were all still numb. For some reason, however, he didn't seem to anticipate that everyone in the audience would be completely frustrated and angry over the limited number of indictments handed down.

Given this opportunity to speak, there a predictable backlash by many of the family members who were not shy about telling the Attorney General exactly what they were thinking. Perhaps none of them made a more poignant statement than the man who shouted out from the very back of the room, near one of the curtained windows, which he had drawn back to expose a large portion of the glass and sash.

"I've got a few things to say to you," the man began. "Number one on the list, you have a lot of nerve bringing us into this building. As I sit in my chair and look around, I see six windows behind me that are nailed shut. *Nailed shut!*" Then he stood up and pointed, "And there's only one exit out of here. You probably didn't notice that, but many of us did. Because it's all the way across the room, if a fast-moving fire were to break out right now, I wouldn't be able to get out. After what you've brought us here to tell us, that's a lot of nerve."

In a room filled not only with the victim's families, but various Rhode Island officials, state police and fire marshals, this man doesn't stop. He proceeds to point out every possible fire hazard imaginable.

"Now," the man announced when he was finished, "I'm going to go out to my truck, I'm going to get my screw driver and I'm going to unlock all the windows in this room."

On his way out, he passes a State Trooper and stops, asking him, "Are you going to stop me?" The officer actually went outside with him and came back with his own screwdriver. Together, the two of them worked unsealing the windows until everyone could be opened.

That pretty much set the tone for the rest of us, and it started with parents of victims speaking and sharing their personal grief and concern over accountability and justice, or lack thereof.

All the while, I'm sitting there wondering if I would be able to hold my tongue. I've always been one to speak my mind. Though others might say that I have a big mouth, I won't argue semantics. I had gone to this meeting to represent Fred, but I had something I wanted to say on behalf of myself as a survivor, and I'll be damned if I was going to sit there silently and not say anything.

When it came around to me, I looked directly at Patrick Lynch and said, "You stand here and tell me that survivors don't matter, and we don't count. I have burns on 40% of my body. I can't play with my kids. I can't do all the things I used to do with them before the fire. Tell me something, do you play sports and games with your kids?" I didn't wait for him to respond in anyway. "You can. I can't. And you're going to tell me that I don't count. None of the survivors count."

When I was done, there was a smattered of applause and people shouting out various exclamatory remarks. Patrick Lynch didn't know what to say. If he had conceived of some politically correct retort, he kept it to himself. It was as if everything I said, everything that everyone in that room said that afternoon, came as a complete surprise to the Attorney General. He really seemed to have no idea that the three measly indictments might generate this kind of reaction from us. That always struck me as odd.

After the meeting, I was still very emotionally charged. I was consumed with so much anger and rage that I was shaking. As soon as I got into my car the first tears started to fall, and before I could make it home I was crying in earnest. I had to pull over into the parking lot of the Christmas Tree Shop nearby, where I turned the car off and balled my eyes out.

It was at that point, drained and tired, tired of everything, I said out loud, *God, that's it. I'm done. This is yours. You don't want to take this away from me, well then I'm going to find another way to deal with* it.

I don't know exactly what I meant by that when I said it, but the outburst left me with a sense of peace, and from that day on I never again felt the depth of anger that I had experienced that day and in the days prior. Some people may not believe that. It's hard for me to believe myself. I was so exhausted from being angry all the time that it was a relief not to have that weight on my shoulders anymore. I felt so much better about myself for it. The anger changed me, it distorted my personality. In a lot of ways the internal damage that the anger did to me was much worse than anything the fire did to the outside of my body. I would never want to have that burden back again.

I used to indulge my mind in vengeful and violent fantasies. I replayed many scenarios in my head about how I wanted to hurt the people who hurt me. I can remember sitting around the dinner table at night with my family talking about how we could torture The Station bouncer and club owners for what they did? We came up with some that could have been used in a *Saw* movie. I never acted on them, of course, but it's scary when you stop and look at yourself and ask, *is that something that I'm really capable of doing?*

We've all heard of serious crimes committed by people who were least suspected. I was terrified, thinking that I could become one of those people. *There had to be another way*, I thought. I didn't like the person I had become. I wasted a lot of precious time being angry and it didn't want to do it anymore.

It was not out of anger that I would later attend the subsequent court hearings of these three men and give a victim's impact statement. Throughout the entire legal process, regardless of how it might turn out, I just wanted to be there to keep Fred's memory alive. That's really all it was ever about for me. I couldn't control who the state chose to indict. My personal goal was for people to walk out of the courtroom having realized that Fred was an incredible person, and that multiple acts of stupidity and negligence had cost a really great man his life.

By the end of it all, I felt confident that I got this point across to both attorney general Lynch and the trial justice, Superior Court Judge Francis J. Darigan, Jr., both of whom later phoned me and told me that they knew I didn't like the outcome, but they had heard every single word I said. That was good to know. It made me feel better because my message was getting across.

But getting back to that day, December 9, 2003, after we had been informed by the attorney general about the indictments, Daniel Biechele, Jeffrey Derderian and Michael Derderian were formally indicted. They were charged with 200 counts each of involuntary manslaughter, two per death because they were indicted under two separate theories of manslaughter. The first was *criminal negligence manslaughter*, which results when the accused ignores the bodily risk to others and death results. The second, *misdemeanor manslaughter*, results from a lesser crime in which death results.

The prosecution seemed satisfied and proud of themselves, boasting a 177-page indictment against the three defendants, one of the largest a state court has ever handled. But the fact that no other individuals, state or city official would face prosecution could not be hidden. It could have been a 10,000 page document, it wouldn't have been enough.

The indictment had been handed down earlier that morning before Superior Court Judge Netti C. Vogel at the Kent County Courthouse in Warwick and immediately sealed. Attorney General Patrick Lynch then arranged the meeting with the victim's families at the West Valley Inn.

By 2 p.m., the three defendants and their lawyers were inside the third-floor courtroom of Judge Vogel. There was plenty of media presence when the judge announced the arraignment of Biechele and the Derderians. Each of them pleaded not guilty to all counts and bail was set.

Each count carried a 30-year penalty, but what all of them still did not seem to understand was that it was not the length of the document or the sentences given to Biechele and the Derderians that mattered.

"We can't provide all the answers to the families," Patrick Lynch told the press afterward. "We can't indict just to please."

When asked why others, such as Jack Russell and public safety directors were not named, he said, "The evidence, facts and law were presented and the grand jury indicted three people."

Simple, straightforward, even logical, but not acceptable. It was not acceptable to me that a jury could come to this decision and it was unacceptable that an attorney general who would go along so easily with their finding.

Biechele posted $10,000, the Derderians $5,000 each, and they were all released. But first, they left the courthouse for processing, fingerprinting and mug shots at the West Warwick police station.

Later that afternoon, Patrick Lynch held a press conference at the Rhode Island National Guard headquarters in Cranston, where daily briefings has been held since the investigation began. The attorney general indicated that further indictments could be made if more information came to light, but he would not speculate any further.

> **December 11, 2003**
> *Freddy, on December 9, 2003 three men (Jeffrey and Michael Derderian and the band manager) were charged with 200 counts for this awful tragedy. This brings some justice for your death but it's not enough. I have been so sick and depressed since that meeting I just lost it and realized I have no strength or energy left to fight this and am leaving this up to God. It's his call and he is the only one who can make things right. I love you Freddy and miss you so much it is not easy living without you. Even though we were only together for 9 months it felt like a lifetime because you wiped away 13 years of heartache and I think I knew from the moment I met you that you were the one I was supposed to spend the rest of my life with. We may not be together physically but I know you will never leave my side and whatever strength you have I could use some help with from time to time. My heart breaks for Brandon and I apologize for not being able to help but right now I cannot handle anything more. I will always keep in touch with him and Nicole to make sure they are all right and let them know I will always be their friend. I had such dreams about you and I know it's all gone this is not like a break up that we can work out I don't get the chance to make this right at least not now but I will one day when we are together again. Good night my love sleep well. May God rest your soul.*

I was not sure how I was going to make it through the holidays. I wanted it to be the very best Christmas my children ever had, but at the same time I was wishing I could just sleep right through it. It seemed so wrong to be celebrating when I felt like it was all a lie, so I did what I could do, and everything I thought I should do, and I wound up merely going through the motions. I thought everyone was expecting me to be happy, happy to be alive, happy to be with my family, and I was both of those things, but all I wanted to do was cry. I didn't though.

I remember sitting at the table Christmas day with my family and wondering if this was really happening. Was I really here, without Fred beside me? I felt so alone, even with my children and my entire family around me. Somehow I got through the entire day, manufacturing a smile for everyone at all the right times. I may as well have been wearing a mask. I just didn't want to disappoint Alex and Nicholas, or completely ruin Christmas for them by letting them know how sad I really was.

Christmas has always been a special time for me and my family. It was the one day when we were sure to be all together. For anyone who was away, they were there in spirit, and no one was forgotten. I almost didn't make it this year, and nobody wanted to mention anything about Fred because they were afraid it would upset me too much. There were a lot of related topics that my family seemed to avoid for the same reason, and even the ones they were unsure about they made sure they steered clear of them as well. Nobody said much of anything that first Christmas after the fire. To this day, the holidays don't mean as much to me as they used to because it just seems as if everyone has lost sight of what the day really means. I know that sounds cliché, and I used to scoff when I used to hear people say things like that myself, but it suddenly rang so true for me. It's just not about what gifts to buy and stressing over making everyone happy. It's about gathering with family and friends and celebrating life, and if this is something that is too unrealistic to do more often, once a year should not be a problem for anybody.

December 29, 2003

Freddy Christmas has come and gone without you it was awful. I made it through the day because of my family but my heart breaks every time I think of you. It is almost 2004 and I cannot stand the thought of another year without you. WHY DID YOU HAVE TO GO? I need you here with me. In the car tonight Nick was talking about you saying

*what a great dad you would have been for them,
you would have played sports with them and been
there for important moments in their life (not like
his father who sleeps and never does anything
with them anymore). They love you so much and
were looking forward to spending their life with
you too. I didn't realize until tonight that they are
missing the same future I was dreaming about for
you and me. Alex and Nick said that if we had
married they would like to have called you dad (I
believe that is something that would have made
you proud that is what I told them) We all love
and miss you so much it just doesn't seem real. I
am going out with Deb and Ray for New Year's
Eve but it will never be the same without you.
Remember last year at JR's how that big girl kept
getting in your face don't worry honey no one will
ever take my place you are all mine for the rest of
your life. I doesn't seem possible that it is coming
up on 1 year since this tragedy nothing seems real
to me. I sometimes find myself wanting to call you
and need to tell you something but then I remember you're not there for me to call so I can only
say a prayer to you and hope you hear me. I love
you so much and cannot accept your death I don't
want to I need you here with me and the boys
PLEASE COME HOME FREDDY you have been
gone too long I miss our special times together I
miss being close to you and having your arms
around me. Good night for now I will go to bed
dreaming about you and wishing I could hold you
close but instead I have the teddy bear you gave
me for Valentine's Day (2/14/03) and it has your
scent on it so I can go to sleep hugging you. Good
Night my love sleep well and rest in peace.*

On January 6, 2004, the last hospitalized survivor of The
Station Nightclub Fire returned home for the first time in ten
months and seventeen days. Joe Kinnan, 34, left Spaulding
Rehabilitation hospital, where he had been since July 23rd. Joe

was arguably the most severely injured survivor, but to anyone who knows him he is truly an inspiration. He was horribly burned. He lost his fingers and much of his nose and ears to the heat and flames. He endured more than thirty operations at Mass General alone in the first five months following the blaze. Yet in spite of his disfigurement and physical limitations, Joe is a person with an incredibly positive outlook on life.

His return home was significant to all of us, as well as Joe. We were all very happy for him and proud.

January 9, 2004

Freddy, I cannot say happy New Year to you or give you anything to fix this but I hope just knowing how much I will always love you will help. You are forever in my thoughts and always in my heart and dreams. You mean the world to me. Yesterday I was interviewed by Rolling Stone Magazine *(did you ever dream) anyway they are going to publish the issue for the 1st year anniversary of the fire. I am also going to be in* The New England Journal of Medicine *(they are publishing my whole medical case) and then there will be a story about my recover in* Advance Magazine. *Freddy I never wanted to be famous I only wanted to find true love and I did with you. I am beginning to believe you came into my life for a reason and maybe your job was done when God took you but why did it have to be so tragic? I am going through so much physically and emotionally I need your help to get through all this. In March I will be undergoing the biggest surgery of my life to reconstruct what I lost in the fire. They will be taking three ribs to form the cartilage of the ear and then a skin graft from my leg to cover the ear and fix it all in one surgery. Then I will go back into the OR a few months later for the second part of the procedure to separate the ear from my head and put pins behind the ear so it will be away from my head then a few months later I go back in for any final touchups. Please be there for me*

through all of this I don't think I could do it with-
out you by my side. Make sure the doctors and
nurses are doing their jobs in the OR right ok. I
love you and will be counting on you to help me
get through all of this. Sweet dreams my love
sleep well.

January 10, 2004
Freddy, last night I went to JR's with Gayle,
Karina, Deb and Ann we had a great time. Back-
lash was playing and I talked to Bobby (lead
singer) he was so nice and compassionate about
what happened to us. He called me on stage and
told the crowd our story (they went wild cheering
me on and wishing me the best) then dedicated an
original song to us. I wish you were here to see all
of this. Me and the boys are going to Deb and
Ray's house tonight to watch the Patriot's playoff
game. I know how much you love the Jets and we
do but I also like to Patriots I hope that doesn't
upset you too much. I love you and will write
again soon. Forever yours.

February 11, 2004
Hi Freddy time is going by so fast without you. I
went to Florida with the kids last week it was fun
but all I could think about was being with you and
how much fun we could have had. Freddy do you
still love me? I never dream about you anymore
and that scares me because I don't want you out
of my life please don't leave me alone I need you
more than ever. You are my best friend and the
one I need to talk to. I still need you so much and
maybe that is too much for you I hope not. These
next couple of week are going to be worse than
anything please stay with me don't leave me
alone. I love you forever Freddy.

CHAPTER 15   ANNIVERSARY

February 15, 2004
Hi Freddy, I didn't write to you yesterday because it was just too much for me to handle. God I want you back and miss our time together. WHY Freddy? I realized something today you are the reason I have been able to handle all of this you found a positive in every negative. Before I met you I would never have been able to handle this situation but now it seems to just happen and before you know it the problem isn't that bad and I just say I am still alive and that is all that matters. The only tough part is doing this without you physically here. Thank you for helping me sometimes I feel like I have lost you altogether but then something will happen and I know you are with me. I talked to your sister Nancy today it felt good because I had not talked to her since November. I am sure this is very hard for her talking to me but she assures me we will always be friends I hope so she is my link to you and your past. All I have are the 9 wonderful months we spent together making each other happy in so many ways. I will be writing to you a lot this week. It is coming up on the one year anniversary of the fire. It just doesn't seem possible that I haven't been with you all that time. I want to feel your arms around me and your kisses everywhere. Please love me no matter what I look like I feel so ugly all the time and worry that you don't want me anymore because of what I look like. Even though I look ugly I am still me and miss all of our crazy time together. Stay with me always. I LOVE YOU ALWAYS

The word anniversary sounds too much like a celebration, but February 20, 2004 was a special day that could not go by without a special observance. I don't know about the other survivors, but I felt a mounting dread the entire week leading up to it. The physical and emotional scars had begun healing, but the pain and trauma was as fresh as it had been fifty-two weeks before. I couldn't believe a whole year had passed.

There were many remembrances, tributes and ceremonies, both public and private, all around the state to mark the year anniversary of the fire. They were too numerous to mention, so I'll mention just one which struck an intimate cord with me. That same week, a Station fire memorial garden was unveiled during the Rhode Island Spring Flower & Garden Show, which opened on February 17 at the Rhode Island Convention Center in Providence. It may sound like a generic tribute, and to others it undoubtedly was, but to me it was more. This special tribute garden was named, "In the Arms of Angels," in honor of the 100 victims of the Station Fire.

Ken Quaranto, a Warwick landscaper, who was also the chairperson of the flower show committee of the Rhode Island Nursery & Landscape Association, spearheaded the memorial garden tribute project. Volunteers from the group's four hundred members planted a hundred white tulips, each bearing the name of a victim, as well as a hundred bleeding hearts, two white dogwoods, rosemary and roses. There was a figure of an angel spreading its wings inside a reflecting pool.

Donations from twenty area nurseries and other businesses helped make the tribute possible. A granite marker was provided by a Georgia company.

The Station Family Fund was set up to be the beneficiary of all donations from visitors to the garden. The providers of the angel and marker offered to donate the items for use in any permanent memorial site that was chosen. The Station Fire Memorial Foundation, a separate group headed by its president, Kimberly Jalette, was seeking to find just such a place for the memorial. While the West Warwick site of the fire remains in legal dispute, a small homemade trellis bearing crosses for each of the hundred victims was put in place and an anniversary prayer service was conducted, organized by the West Warwick Fraternal Order of Eagles.

February 18, 2004

Hi Freddy. I just need to talk to you for awhile. I cannot believe it has been one year since I have seen you, kissed you, hugged you or made love with you. I am so scared that at some point I am going to crack and then what will I do when I have to face the reality that you are really gone and I won't ever get the chance to do all those things with you again. My head is so messed up right now and I am trying to be so strong and positive for everyone I don't want to let them down anymore they have all been through so much. Do you have the slightest clue about how much I am hurting and missing you? Please don't leave my side I need to always feel you with me you are the one making me strong. Please help me get through the next couple of days and maybe on Saturday I will feel like maybe this was all supposed to mean something and you and God will guide me in the right direction. You will be my guiding light always. I am sure Brandon needs you so much so maybe me and him can share your loving spirit. I will write again tomorrow night after the remembrance service at the Rhodes-on - the-Pawtuxet service and let you know how it went. Please sleep well and God rest your soul. I LOVE YOU ALWAYS.

On Thursday, February 19, 2004, Governor Carcieri held a remembrance at Rhodes-On-The-Pawtuxet, a popular and historic reception hall in Cranston. Financed from the governor's contingency budget, "The Station Fire Remembrance" was free and open to the public. Not all the survivors and family members who could attend did so, but many did, and more than nine hundred people showed up that night. I was among them with members from my family and Fred's family.

The event featured, among other tributes, a row of tables with pictures and mementos of each fire victim. These items would later be placed on display at the State House for three weeks before being stored permanently among the state's official archives. The entire facility was decorated with homemade butterflies created by school children from around the state. These colorful winged creatures were dually representative as a symbol of hope and renewal. In keeping with this theme, The Roger Williams Park Zoo in Providence dedicated its butterfly gardens to The Station victims and survivors. Among the songs played and performed at the anniversary remembrance reception, a young girl sang Mariah Carey's, "Butterfly." The lyrics were poignant and personal.

> *I can't pretend these tears*
> *Aren't overflowing steadily*
> *I can't prevent this hurt from*
> *Almost overtaking me*
> *But I will stand and say goodbye*
> *Blindly I imagined I could*
> *Keep you under glass*
> *Now I understand to hold you*
> *I must open up my hands and watch you rise.*

Reverend Robert Marciano, a Warwick police and fire chaplain, asked the gathering to draw strength from the Rhode Island state motto: HOPE.

A bell echoed one hundred times, a solitary methodical resonating moan for each victim.

It was on this one year anniversary of the fire that I had my only other personal encounter with the bouncer who changed my life instantly and permanently. Considering all of the people that were in attendance that night, I never expected to run into this man.

While this bouncer, who would not allow Fred and me to leave the burning nightclub, escaped completely unscathed himself, his wife, Kelly, did not. She was at Shriners in a room close to mine while I was there. She was also in a coma. When her husband came to visit, he often appeared to be drunk, loud and out of control. My family witnessed this behavior from him many times, not knowing then who he was or what he did. The hospital staff would have to babysit him while he was there, and generally keep an eye on him in case he caused a major disturbance.

On at least one occasion, he went too far. My family was gathered outside my room conferring with one of my doctors. This bouncer was within earshot of their conversation and overheard the doctor explaining to my brother and sister a surgical procedure that he was going to attempt in the hope of saving my hands.

The bouncer turned around to Jim and Stephanie and said, "Why are you letting them bother. She's going to be useless and good for nothing either way."

My brother went absolutely wild when he heard this, and flew into a rage. Security had to be called. It got ugly. It was truly astounding how someone could be so indifferent and cruel toward people who were suffering along with their loved ones who were so badly injured, and all on account of his actions. His wife ended up passing away, becoming the 98th victim of The Station Fire. And while his own sorrow and guilt may have contributed to his callous behavior, it was completely inexcusable to act the way he did.

I happened to know who his daughters were from other events, and I noticed them right away when I walked into the Rhodes-On-The-Pawtuxet banquet room. They were alone when I saw them and I didn't think anything more of it. Then, as I was taking my jacket off, I turned around to put it on the back of my seat when I was startled by this large man who was suddenly standing beside me. I flinched slightly and lost my balance, dropping back into my chair, which fortunately happened to be right behind me or would have fallen to the floor. I quickly stood back up, and this man just stood there, towering over me. I looked him in the eye and said, "Oh my God! It's you!"

"Yeah," was all that he said. It seemed as if he stared back at me for a long time before turning away. But I had detected a little smirk and sense of pride about him, as if reveling in his notoriety and the affect it had on me.

I relived the moment, almost exactly a year ago, when this person was blocking the door Fred and I wanted to go through to escape the spreading fire. Now, here he was again, like grim death. More recently, I've come to believe that's exactly what he was. He may very well have been wearing a Grim Reaper's hood. Out of respect to his family, who are innocent in all this, I will not use his real name. Instead, in keeping with this image I have of him as an agent of death, I will refer to him simply as Grim.

Through the years, this person has always been quite symbolic to me, representing all the remaining fear and hate and guilt that I have inside me. I've made him a personification of the fire. A physical, living, breathing incarnate of the mindless rampaging flames that swallowed The Station and tried to consume everyone under its roof. The way it appeared, at least, this person didn't work for the club, he worked for the fiery beast. He was feeding us alive to it, steering us directly into its gnashing, flaming teeth. While I could not confront the fire itself, this man was real. Before I die I would like nothing more than to be given another opportunity to stand before this person and tell him that my life was worth saving. Then I could walk away *from him* and put the fire behind me for good. He had been so out of it during that entire year after the fire that he may not even remember the things he did or said. He may not even recognize me. The fire didn't care what it did to me either, but personally I need to do this.

It hasn't happened yet, but it will. When the time is right, I will face the Grim Reaper again, this figurative manifestation just as surely as the real thing.

There were other survivors who have given similar accounts as me, being prevented from escaping though the backstage door by a bouncer who was upholding "company policy." I later met one of these survivors. His family had organized a fund-raiser for him, and who should show up at the event but Grim himself. If this wasn't bad enough, he proceeded to brag about the fact that he had prevented people from getting out of the nightclub as the fire spread. Again, he was not in a right state of mind, for sure, but he was lucky that no one beat the crap out of him. The father of this particular survivor, while at a fundraiser for his critically injured son, had to be restrained from doing just that to Grim.

Just incomprehensible.

And then later, when I began to step out with other survivors, Grim would turn up at the places where we would meet. There were certain areas inside the clubs where we would all congregate, usually very close to one of the exit doors, and Grim was often nearby. At one particular club, the owner made sure he kicked Grim out before we arrived. It wasn't as if he was harassing us so much as his presence was tormenting. Drunk or not, he knew the affect he had on us and it didn't matter to him one bit. He actually seemed to enjoy it.

For me personally, the confrontation I had with Grim at the anniversary event marred an otherwise beautiful evening and a touching memorial service.

There were other less appreciated anniversary tributes that I thought did more harm than good, and only served to rip open old wounds.

For some reason, the Derderians felt the need to contact the media via e-mail to express their sorrow and offer prayers to the families and survivors. The prepared statement was sent to a former colleague and friend who worked with Jeffrey Derderian at Channel 6 in Providence.

This was something the brothers had to have done for their own benefit, because the rest of us could have done without hearing what had been on their minds during the past year.

Likewise, Jack Russell made a public announcement when he spoke to a Massachusetts radio station. He claimed that he only agreed to go on the air in order to increase awareness of The Station Family Fund and generate contributions made on its behalf. He also said that he had been invited to attend some of the anniversary events in Rhode Island, but thought it wise to just stay home in California.

When asked about the anger that had been directed toward him and Great White, the band he founded in 1978, Russell said, "I can't fault them for being upset," then went on to basically recite the mantra of the current generation, *It is what is*, thereby removing himself completely from any of the responsibility.

"If they want to blame the band," he said, "and they want to blame me, if it makes them feel better, that's OK. Not everyone is going to understand. Some people won't see past the first spark."

He actually said that, as if he thought that it was unreasonable for people to hold him accountable for what goes on at his own concert. It's difficult for a lot of people today to even recall what life was like prior to that first spark. So much had changed for so many of us, we have been forced to adopt a whole new way of living. Jack Russell's life hardly changed, besides not being welcomed in Rhode Island.

He even compared the fire to a plane crash, admitting that, "There were a lot of things that went wrong."

His ordering Daniel Biechele to set off pyrotechnics inside The Station was one of those things. The Rhode Island Attorney

General seemed to be the only person who didn't see anything past that first spark.

At the end of the interview, Russell broke down, and I cannot question the sincerity in his sorrow. However, drunk drivers who survive car accidents that kill others are sorrowful as well, but it doesn't excuse the crime or magically purge them of all social responsibility just because they are sorry.

CHAPTER 16   LETTERS TO FRED

I tried to show courage, but my outward demeanor belied my fear, anger and frustration. I concealed these emotions and projected a stronger self-image for others. It was my loss of Fred more than anything that continued to haunt my soul, and I spent a lot of time writing diary-like letters expressing my feelings and love for Fred. This went on for many months and years after the fire. In some sense, I suppose I was in denial. I had been writing to him as if he was alive, and that was my way of avoiding the truth. Looking back, I don't think it ever actually dawned on me that Fred really wasn't coming home until the first year anniversary came and went. I had never gotten a chance to say good-bye to Fred at his funeral and mourn his death. It was still in the hospital, in a coma, when Fred was laid to rest and I lacked the closure I needed to move on.

I came to understand that there had only been a handful of victims who were able to have an open casket funeral, and Fred was one of them. Somehow, he was hardly burned at all. One ear had been slightly singed, as were portions of his mustache and hair. The bodies of other victims lying on top of him preserved his flesh from the touch of the flames. Smoke inhalation claimed his life as it had so many others. While some victims had to be identified by tattoos, jewelry or dental records, I took some comfort in Fred's body having been spared from destruction by the fire. I just wished I could have seen him one last time. When his body was recovered, the watch he was wearing was cracked and had stopped at 11:13. I have that watch in my possession today.

My sons had attended Fred's services and were amazed how many people were on hand to pay their respects at his wake. A line to get into the funeral home was wrapped around the building. Five books of condolence were filled with names of the visitors, including members of local rock bands. One in particular, Backlash, Fred had gotten to know on a personal level. He went to see them play whenever he could, and after we started dating I would go with him. Eventually we all became close and my friendship with the members from the group continued after I got home from the hospital. I can't say enough about them. They've always been there for me, as well as the other Station Fire survivors, playing at all the fund-raisers and just being a source of strength and support. Whatever is needed, they would do it, as so many other local bands and national acts have been doing, and continue to do. The Rhode Island music scene has always been a very close knit community. Everyone knows everyone else. They become like family to one another, and in times of crisis they rally around you.

In the beginning, it wasn't just my letters to Fred and my constant thoughts of him that held me back from working through my grief and getting over Fred. I also made a habit out of visiting the site of the fire every week. After my physical therapy on Thursdays I would stop at a Dunkin Donuts and buy a small coffee with milk and two sugars – just the way Fred liked it – and then drive to West Warwick. I would leave the coffee on the spot where I believed Fred had taken his last breath. I had no real way of knowing, of course, the site had been leveled flat and transformed into a makeshift memorial ground. But I thought I had a pretty good recollection of the layout of The Station, and assumed that Fred was not far behind me and the pileup at the front door. I just felt closer to Fred there than I did at the cemetery. But I'm sure now that this was also just another form of denial. I didn't want to believe that Fred was dead and buried.

But then, in February 2004, at a memorial service at St. Ann's Church in Cranston, that all changed. I was with my family and Fred's family attending an anniversary mass. It had been a year since I'd last seen Fred, touched him, heard him laugh, but it was as if it had all just happened. For me, it was still 2003. I honestly kept expecting to see a casket being wheeled down the aisle with Fred inside. When it never came, this must have created some kind of crisis in my mind. I suddenly became overwhelmed, crying inconsolably, and I had to leave. I remember I kept asking Rene and Brian, "This is real, isn't it? He's really, really gone?"

For me, this memorial service *was* Fred's funeral. I was finally able to say good-bye to Fred and resolve much of the grief I had been carrying for the past year. It was painful, but it freed me from the confines of the past, and helped push me forward so that I could move on with my life.

Though there were constant reminders which forced me to confront the reality of Fred's death, this was a defining moment in that realization. One painful example occurred when the dating service that had brought us together contacted me and inquired about the progress of our relationship. From the beginning, they would e-mail us periodically for updates, but for the past year I did not respond to any of their requests. Once, Fred told me that he had informed them that he was going to propose to me, so they knew we were serious. What they apparently didn't know was that Fred had been killed in The Station Fire. Of the hundred of e-mails in my inbox, which I discovered when I was finally able to use my computer again, there was one from the dating service, and I opened every single one but not the one from HipDates.com. I didn't delete it either, however, and then one day I somehow managed to muster up enough strength and courage to read the message and write back to them. I was difficult, but it was also liberating to admit to others, and myself, what had happened:

Fred would never be my husband. He died in the fire at The Station on February 20, 2003.

Sometime after I was home, a friend told me that people come into our lives for a reason. To do a job, whatever it may be, to help us, teach us something or improve ourselves in some way, and when this job is done, they go away.

At first, I dismissed this as just a thoughtful statement of sympathy, but the more I considered it the more truth I saw in this philosophy. As painful as a loved one's premature departure from your life can be, what they came into your life to do will last forever and you're changed for the better as a result. It made all the sense in the world. I truly believe that my path crossed with Fred's so that he could show me that there are men who treat women with respect and dignity, and even put them on a pedestal. It was something I did not think was possible, at least in my case, until I met Fred. Before him, I never felt I was important enough to anyone to be made a priority. My self-esteem was low and my self-loathing was high, and Fred changed all that in the short time we had together. How could Fred's emergence into my world at that time be seen as anything other than a godsend?

It was also why it was so difficult for me to let go. I may have been able to move on, but I had nowhere to go.

February 29, 2004

I am so depressed. I hate the weekends. They make me realize just how alone and lonely I really am. I miss you so fucking much. Why did you leave? No matter how mad I am at you for leaving me alone again I still love you so very much and miss you like hell.

March 8, 2004

Hi Freddy, I went out Friday night with my cousin Deb and friends Rene and Liv met us out to see Backlash at JR's it was fun but I miss being there with you. I also was with a friend Richard he lost his wife in the fire. I am so confused about everything I guess I am so lonely I wish he liked me in more than just a friendship way but how could he ever want someone who looks like me? On the other hand I think I am just so lonely that I wish it was possible. I am sorry I don't mean to talk to you about all this but I need your help I am so alone and lonely you left me and I don't want to be alone even though I have said I would be ok for the rest of my life. You are my one and only true love and no one could ever change that I hope you understand how much I love you but am so afraid of spending the rest of my life alone. I realize this is not a good time in my life to be thinking about all of this but I cannot help it. I miss being close to someone and being loved by someone other than my kids and family. You only get one great love in this lifetime and you are so it for me but I am so lonely please don't be mad at me for feeling this way I so badly want you back here loving me and making me laugh and being with my children who love you so much. I miss you and will love you always.

April 6, 2004

Freddy it has been awhile so many things have happened. I had surgery to start reconstructing my left ear that I lost in the fire. Dr. Mack Cheney at the Mass Eye and Ear Infirmary is doing the procedure that will take three surgeries to complete. I wish you were here with me in person I believe you are with me in spirit and I will have to accept that you will never be here physically to comfort me through all of this. I can sometimes feel your strength and positive attitude so that is what helps me get through all of this and the love of my kids and family. Please don't ever leave me alone I need your love and support always and forever so I hope you don't mind because when it is my time I plan on spending eternity with you. Good rest your soul my love and never ever forget the love we have for each other.

April 12, 2004

Happy Easter Freddy. It is the day after and for some reason I feel so depressed. WHY I am tired of feeling this way. My kids have every right in the world to hate me and I think my son Nick is tired of it too. He always wants to be at my sisters with his cousins because I cannot do much of anything with them poor Alex what a great kid he has been and so good to me they don't deserve this. Help me be strong Freddy for some reason I don't feel it anymore. My weight is bothering me and it doesn't matter if I eat or not I am just gaining weight and feeling fat and even uglier than I am. I am not sure even you could have handled what I am going through no matter how much you loved me. I hope I am wrong and want to believe we could have overcome all of this. I love you very much and miss you even more.

May 9, 2004

Hi Freddy, it is Mother's Day and I am nothing but depressed. So many things are wrong and I keep trying to help make them right but no one seems to care. I love my family more than any-

*thing and I just want to give back what they gave
to me. I need to find the strength to just stop caring about everyone else and just worry about me
and the boys. My cousin Debbie says it just isn't
my nature to not want to help and make things
right she may be right but I mentally cannot handle this anymore I am exhausted from all of this. I
guess because everyone went through so much
with me because of the fire I feel like I owe them
something back but I just cannot do this anymore.
Thanks for listening to me and my problems I wish
you were here with me then maybe it wouldn't
seem so bad. I hope when this is over you and I
will be together for all eternity. I love you so
much and cannot stand the pain anymore of missing you it isn't getting any easier only harder.*

June 10, 2004
*Hi Freddy, I could really use your strength right
about now. I feel like I could run away with my
two kids and never look back and that makes me
feel so guilty because of how good my family has
been to me. I miss you and sometimes get mad at
you for leaving me here to deal with this all alone.
I wish I could be given some kind of answer as to
WHY this had to happen to us after we finally
found happiness and were looking forward to a
long life together. I know I am not supposed to
question God but I cannot help it anymore it
seems nothing ever goes right for me for very long
or I am not allowed to find happiness ever in my
personal life. I will always love you and miss you.*

June 20, 2004
*Happy Father's Day Freddy. I went to the site and
left you some roses what a switch me giving you
roses just like you always gave them to me. I will
do my best to make sure I put roses there all the
time you deserve so much more than that but it is
the best I can do because you left me 16 months*

ago it hurts that I couldn't say good-bye even though I still am not ready to let you go I don't think I ever will love anyone the way I love you. I hope you can feel the love I have for you and that gives you some comfort in heaven. I love you and always will.

June 27, 2004
Hi Freddy, today we had a birthday party for Alex he is 11 years old and you would be very proud of him. He misses you very much and wishes you could be here to watch him grow and most of all play baseball. I am having another surgery on 6/30/04 to hopefully fix my left index finger I am so tired of this I just want to be better. Please watch over me in the O.R. and say a prayer that the doctor is able to fix it. I love you still so very much you are my guardian angel and always my knight in shining armor. Forever yours.

July 4, 2004
Happy fourth Freddy. I am having such a shitty day and I don't want to feel this way all I want to do is cry. I cannot type or write the right way because of the surgery on my left hand I cannot enjoy anything anymore everything sucks I have been so bitchy to my parents for no reason at all. I wish you were here with me. I Love You always.

July 11, 2004
Hi Freddy, I feel so sad today. Yesterday my friends Stephanie and Andrew got married and it was so beautiful I couldn't help but wonder what it would have been like for us. I miss you every day and cannot stop thinking about us and all of the good times we had. I will never understand why you were taken away when you we so full of life and we had finally found happiness with each other my heart is breaking I don't want to be alone anymore. I love you always. Please watch

*over me tomorrow I am having more surgery on
my left ear.*

February 14, 2005
*Hi Freddy it has been a long time since I have
written in my journal to you but that doesn't me I
have forgotten about you it is the exact opposite
you are in my thoughts every day and every night.
Especially today on Valentine's Day I miss you
and wish like crazy we were spending this and
every other day together. You are still my knight
in shining armor. It is almost two years and I
cannot even begin to tell you how much has happened and what it has been like without you. Next
week Feb 24 I am having dinner with our favorite
band TESLA can you believe it. I have become
friends with the band through some friends and
Troy who is the drummer has called my house and
it was the greatest experience I just wish you were
here for all of this. I know you will always be with
me is spirit some days it seems like I can feel you
presence which brings me comfort especially at
night when I miss you even more. There are times
I feel like I can actually feel you touching me or
sitting on my bed with me. Maybe it is just wishful
thinking but I hope it's more than that. It seems
like forever since that awful night when all we did
was go out for a good time. I never got to say
good-bye to you and don't know if I ever really
can. You're in my heart always and will have my
love for eternity.*

CHAPTER 17   MONEY MATTERS

During the time of the two year anniversary of the fire, the state of Rhode Island began to tighten its purse strings on money targeted for Station Fire survivors and their families. The reasons included their claim that fewer people than had been predicted had applied for the aid provided by the state's Crime Victims Compensation Fund. The General Treasurer's office, which managed the fund, suggested that even those who have applied usually need less than the full amount available, which was set at $25,000.

Also, because private donations from individuals and businesses were helping those in need, the state seemed to think that its obligation to its citizens did not need to be fulfilled, or at least not "that much."

The Crime Victims Compensation Fund provided money taken from court fees, fines and federal grants and occasionally from state general revenue appropriations. The law regarding disbursement of this money does state that other money received as aid would have to be exhausted before being granted this state money. In that regard, it could be said that the state was acting as a secondary insurer, picking up the tab for what was not covered by the primary insurer. I don't have a problem with that. I realize that this is money that is targeted for *all* people who are the victims of various crimes in the state, not just Station Fire survivors, and that there is only so much to go around. However, if there is money available and it is being held back from those affected by The Station Fire because the state thinks that we've been *taken care of*, that's what I take issue with, because they're wrong. They were telling us we had enough, we were OK. We were not. Not as a whole group. Individually, some were getting by, but you can't say we were OK. None of us were doing as well as we would have been doing if that fire had not occurred.

The state said it had added $800,000 in general revenue to the fund in 2004, then made sure they had that much available for 2005, and on top of that adding another $2.2 million. In addition, $1.1 million in federal money was earmarked for the families. The

$2.2 million, however, was believed not to be needed, and the governor proposed to take it off the table in his budget revision. In the next budget, only $28,000 was proposed for Station survivors because they expected most claims to be paid.

Money may not have been the most important issue in a time like this, but unfortunately it is always a concern, especially when there are children involved. I was one of the lucky ones. I was fully insured by my employer, and as such I qualified for Long Term Disability Benefits, which began on the date of the fire, following a thirty day elimination period, and lasted until I was able to get back to work. The benefits began to be dispersed just before I left Shriners, the amount derived from 60% of my monthly income.

My family had also filed an application with the Rhode Island Medical Assistance Program on my behalf. I became eligible for state financial compensation on March 1, and began receiving $310 per week as well as having health care services available for Nicholas and Alex.

Two years later, the inescapable fact was that many families remained without a second income or with the primary breadwinner unable to work because of their injuries, and had to cope with grave financial difficulties that left them on the verge of homelessness. Federal aid never came, with only 15 survivors qualifying for Social Security benefits. State money was also scant, with what little there was available coming from the Rhode Island Crime Victims Compensation Fund, which began to be disbursed after the December 2003 indictments were handed down. According to figures they provided, by February 2005, 256 people had applied for the aid, with 117 of those given a total sum of $937,799, or an average of around $8,000 each, with other cases still pending approval and disbursement. Even The Station Family Fund coffers, would periodically run dry.

But the music community, its musicians and fans, continued to support their own. On February 28, 2005, a benefit concert was held at the Providence Performing Arts Center. Telsa, headlined the sold out show, which also featured contemporary and legendary rock acts that included Shinedown, Mars Hill, Vanilla Fudge's Carmine Appice and Pat Travers. $100,000 was raised for survivors and their families. The Station Family Fund and the Wake Up To Love foundation co-hosted the charity event.

I attended the concert along with over three hundred other survivors and victim's family members. Local radio station WHJY was always supportive of everything that was done on behalf of people affected by the fire, and they were there for us once again this night. DJ Paul Fuller emceed the event. Many other people and businesses participated to help make this event a tremendous success and a whole lot of fun for those who attended.

Some other events that were taking place around this time seemed to undermine all of the good that was being done. While these things were beyond our control, it was disheartening and maddening.

Marking the end of the second year of the fire, the Derderians made a formal legal request to have all charges against them dropped. Their lawyers alleged that the grand jury was never made aware of a particular FAX, which they not only deemed vital to the case but believed its presentation would have impacted the juror's decisions in favor of their clients. The FAX, sent anonymously to prosecutors by American Foam Corporation salesman Barry Warner, told of his company's policy of withholding from their customers the hazards of its foam products, including flammability dangers.

The Derderians and their lawyers thought this information would somehow instantly absolve them of all responsibility. When this attempt failed, having exhausted their last line of defense against the criminal charges, their next move was to file for personal bankruptcy to safeguard their personal finances from the civil liability suits that were sure to follow.

Maybe Jeffrey and Michael Derderian couldn't protect their asses, so they were going to protect their assets.

There certainly were some asses who seemed to be protected, however, never having been charged or named in criminal indictments. This immunity that extended into the civil arena was most maddening when a year later, on November 18, 2005, the state Fire Marshall was dropped from the civil suit.

March 1, 2005
Freddy this day was right up there with the night of the fire and the day I found out you didn't make it out of the fire. On February 24, 2005 your sister Nancy DePasquale passed away no one seems to

know why. Today was her funeral it hurt so much like losing you all over again. I hope you're both together and have found peace in heaven. She was so special to me and even though we hadn't seen each other in a long time I always knew she was around if I needed a friend. I will miss you Nancy and hopefully you are resting and will find the peace I think you needed so badly since Freddy left this earth. Your children are strong like their mother and seem to have a great many relatives to help them through life but I am sure you know they will always need your guidance and support. How lucky are they to have so many good people as their angels. Freddy please take care of your sister she has had such a hard life and deserves happiness and peace that I know she will find with you in heaven. I can only hope that what I have been told is true that when my time comes we will be together again and for me I will be living my life here knowing that someday I will be with my one true great love you. For now I have work to do on earth and am not ready to leave I hope God grants me enough years to watch my children grow and become good adults then to see them be married and hopefully they will have what you and I didn't. You are in my every waking thought and sleepless nights. I love you always. Rest in peace Nancy I love you.

On March 3, 2005, the U.S. Department of Commerce invited the families of The Station Nightclub Fire to attend a briefing to review a tentative draft report compiled by National Institute of Standards and Technology (NIST) and conducted under the authority of the National Construction Safety Team Act. The goal of the report was to achieve a true, if not better understanding of the February 20, 2003 fire and to make recommendations for improvements in the public safety standards. From the comments made by individuals and organizations at this briefing, changes were made to the draft report and several months later those amendments became part of the final exhaustive examination of the fire. The complete findings were first presented to the families before they were made public, and although much of what was contained inside was not something that was new to any of us, it was disturbing to see the graphic details of the fire recorded the way they were in this highly technical, matter-of-fact, manual-like report. It was more than 400 pages long, and involved the efforts and skills of many people, most notably three individuals with the NIST Building and Fire Research Laboratory, including William Grosshandler, the lead investigator, along with Nelson Bryner and Daniel Madrzykowski. Kenneth Kuntz, who completed the four-member Team, represented the Federal Emergency Management Agency and the U.S. Department of Homeland Security. Their work began on February 27, 2003.

By analyzing interior layout designs of various building models and existing fire codes, as well as public documents, photograph and video images, phone and radio transmissions, personal accounts and witness statements, they were able to determine the movement of smoke and the spread of fire through the nightclub. Independent fire tests on the representative material were particularly informative and shocking. It clearly showed that the fire could have been avoided and that simple safety measures and precautions could have been taken which would have slowed or prevented the fire altogether.

As perhaps overstated already, the cheap foam festooned around the stage and the dance floor should never have been used. But it was, and everything after that happened that night played off that decision. The other major contributing factor was the use and placement of the pyrotechnics, so close to the volatile foam, which made The Station a proverbial recipe for disaster. There were other key ingredients, as well, and this is what this report was supposed to determine.

With so many people jammed inside the building at the time the fire broke out, there was little chance of avoiding a large number of casualties once the fast-moving fire started. The lack of sprinklers and the grandfather clause that kept the owners from having to install them, did not grant them even one additional second to escape.

Since this report is a technical critique of the disaster, what the investigators never speculated was that somewhere inside the club owner's themselves there should have existed a moral responsibility to do everything necessary to protect the well-being of the patrons, even if the law did not require it. That moral responsibility apparently did not exist in either Jeffrey or Michael Derderian. There can be no argument there. The pennies they saved on the foam relative to the number of deaths and injuries that their decision cost in the end is what makes the Derderians liable, at least in my mind. The liability certainly does not stop with them.

I've also already discussed at some length the bouncer who prevented many victims and survivors from getting out of the burning building, but before I go any further I just wanted to make it clear that it has never been my intention to write this book for the purpose of laying blame on anyone and everyone who played a role in the death and destruction that took place that night at The Station. But this is what happened. I can't change any of that. This book is about the only thing there is to live for, hope and love, not hate and revenge.

The fact remains, no state officials, fire or building inspectors, lost their jobs in the wake of this tragedy, even though The Station had been given a passing grade by the fire inspector only three months before it burnt to the ground. With regard to the deadly soundproofing foam around the stage, this was apparently never even noticed by inspectors. Either that or it intentionally had not been cited in any of the three previous inspections that had been conducted since its installation in June 2000. It was the job of the safety inspectors to verify the existence of such material so that it could be removed and avert a disaster.

What's interesting to note is that many people believed that The Station was exempt from sprinkler system requirements because of a ridiculous grandfather clause, when in fact this represented another glaring oversight on the part of building and fire inspectors. When the building had undergone an occupancy change at the time it was converted from a restaurant to a nightclub, this modification actually voided its grandfather exemption from the sprinkler system law. So it was that on the night that my Fred and ninety nine other people were killed, The Station was legally required to have an operating sprinkler system, but did not. This detail was also overlooked by West Warwick fire inspectors.

Would sprinklers have prevented all the deaths and injuries that resulted from the fire that night? Maybe not, but even if it saved just one life it would have been worth it. That life may have been Fred's.

No public officials ever admitted that they screwed up in any way, shape or form. Instead, the response from these municipal departments was exactly what you might expect, akin to closing the barn door after the horse got out, as fire Marshals around the state worked double and triple time to inspect every dive bar and nightclub in the state for safety violations, immediately shutting down many which did not comply. Obviously, changes in fire and building codes needed to be implemented to increase safety, but these inspectors who were going around and kicking down doors like they were super heroes was a joke. What they were really doing was simply their jobs, nothing more. If they had been doing their jobs all along, this catastrophe would not have happened.

When it became painfully apparent that none of these people were going to be held accountable in The Station Fire disaster, it only served to validate the old adage that you can't fight City Hall.

In the end, after all the fact-finding and data-analysis by the NIST and the release of their much-anticipated report, the organization came up with twelve very precise recommendations which they believed would go a very long way to see to it that a similar fire tragedy would never occur in this state again. I won't get into them here, but I will say that they include banning the use of pyrotechnics at all indoor entertainment venues as well as setting and enforcing more stringent occupancy limits and banning all non-fire retardant foam materials from building interiors.

Mind you, these are only recommendations, and in order for them to be of any value to human life, they not only must be adapted into state code law, they must also be strictly enforced. Tragically, the lives and fate of many people would be very different today if these recommendations had been in place on February 20, 2003.

CHAPTER 18   TRYING TO FIND SOME GOOD

By the end of 2005, I was ready to give something back. It didn't exactly know what I had to offer, and it wasn't as if I had been actively seeking out a cause to get behind at the time. It just happened. My good friend, Stephanie Niewola, told me about a campaign she was involved in to help the Smithfield Fire Department raise money for new and upgraded equipment which they desperately needed. As well as being a case manager for Blue Cross, Stephanie was a RN. She worked in the emergency room at Roger Williams Hospital in Providence, where she got to know a lot of the fire fighters. I immediately saw an opportunity for me to thank some of the people who were responsible for giving Alex and Nicholas their mother back. I thought these fire fighters would appreciate being reminded that there were plenty of survivors like me who were alive and happy and productive as a result of their actions. If nothing else, I was living proof what dependable rescue equipment can provide a community.

The first thing we did was arrange a visit to the firehouse so I could talk to the fire fighters personally. Stephanie spoke to the fire chief and told him what I wanted to do. He granted my request to address them and say whatever I wanted.

I wasn't sure how I might be received, and I remember being very nervous. I realized that it would probably be very difficult for some of them to confront a Station Fire survivor, even after all this time. Their department had been one of the first respondents to the scene on February 20, 2003. They had pulled body after body out of the flames and smoldering debris. The death and the suffering they witnessed that night would have overwhelmed anybody. Post traumatic stress, perhaps feelings of guilt for not saving more people, all of these negative effects were very real and weighed heavily on them. I could see it on their faces and in their body language the moment that Stephanie and I arrived that day. There was no hiding my scars. It was difficult for these men and women to even look at me before I ever spoke a word.

I started to think that maybe this wasn't such a good idea. What if they didn't want to hear what I had to say? I began to get an uneasy feeling in the pit of my stomach and I thought I was going to throw up. If I could have made myself disappear at the very moment, I probably would have done it.

Stephanie was up first. She explained the purpose of our visit and why we wanted to help them. For the most part, the fire fighters in the room kept their emotional *and* physical distance, not wanting to stand too close. When Stephanie was finished, the chief stepped in and told them that there was someone else who wanted to say something to them. He added that if anyone felt uncomfortable at any time it would be all right to just get up and leave until I was through. Then he introduced me, and it seemed to get real quiet all at once. I certainly had everyone's attention standing alone before them in the center of the room.

"My name is Gina Russo," I began. "I don't know any of you, but one of you may have saved my life." I told them a little bit about myself and my story of what happened the night of February 20, 2003. I said, "I just need to say thank you to all of you because I don't know who pulled me out."

I told them that everything was going well for me, and I thought it was important for them to know that.

With each sentence I felt more at ease. As I continued, some of them did walk out, but they eventually came back.

"I am very happy," I said. "I take it one day at a time and I'm grateful for every moment. It's like getting a second chance at life, and it was all because of you and people like you who rescued me and others from The Station."

By the time I was through, many of them had tears in their eyes.

Later, as I was preparing to leave, some of the fire fighters came up to me and told me that they had been petrified to meet me because, although they empathized, they could not specifically relate. They had only seen the devastation that night, read the accounts of the living horror the survivors were experiencing in the hospitals, grieving and rehabbing. They had seen my picture and story profiled in *Rolling Stone* magazine. They felt insubstantial next to me, as if I was the embodiment of their failure. It was exactly what I hoping they would not experience.

However, they admitted that after seeing how I looked now, two years later, and hearing me declare how lucky I felt and that I was happy to be alive, it was overwhelming to them. It made them feel good, and proud, to know that they made a difference in someone's life. They thanked *me* for coming. As difficult as it was for me at first, it was just such a satisfying experience to say thank you to someone and have them take it to heart. It is something I'll never forget.

We were able to raise enough money for the Smithfield Fire Department to purchase the equipment they needed. A Poker Night was organized with the help of actor Denis Leary, who grew up in Worcester, MA and plays a fire fighter on TV's *Rescue Me*. It was a lot fun and a big success. Leary was an inspiration to me. He founded his own charity after two of his cousins, both fire fighters, were killed in a Worcester mill fire. Stephanie and I were hoping to continue this work and help other Rhode Island fire departments secure equipment and other fire apparatus, but unfortunately the program never got off the ground the way we had planned. Truth be told, there was a genuine reluctance on the part of many town departments to participate in our program. I'm not exactly sure why, but The Station Family Fund was also hesitant to get involved in such a project, and rightfully so, wanting to focus their efforts and channel all money toward the families of the fire victims and the survivors.

For me, just meeting this one group of fire fighters meant so much. I was glad I was able to reach out, do something useful, something that others could benefit from. It's the kind of thing I hope to continue to do in one form or another in the future. Given the right time and circumstance, I believe there's a lot of good that will come from this tragedy. There are many people, not just survivors, who continue to help a lot of people who are hurting as a result of this catastrophic fire. I was involved in helping accomplish one small thing for a local fire department, but with so many others offering their time and resources to help others, it becomes part of something much bigger than ourselves. And there's nothing more important than that.

While the skill and efforts of my surgeons and therapists made me near whole again physically, healing the psychological scars was a bit trickier. There obviously were some issues that I still needed to work out, but I hadn't had a whole lot of success talking to therapists in the past, and I admit to having even less confidence in them as a result.

The first therapist I spoke to giggled incessantly throughout our first session. Every time I told her something that related to the fire she would literally giggle. It wasn't that she found any of what I said humorous, I could discern that much, but I didn't know what to make of it. I wondered if I had tumbled down a bizarre rabbit-hole and was face to face with the Mad Hatter. She was actually wearing a fashionable bowler type of hat, like the ones Diane Keaton wears. It may even have been made of felt, but I'm sure the material is no longer cured with mercury, a process which released poisonous fumes that often caused neurological damage to early hat makers, and allegedly to some wearers, making them appear disturbed or mentally confused. Still, I was half expecting to be served tea and have a Cheshire cat jump on my lap and whisper in my ear.

I could only assume that this woman, who seemed to be an otherwise qualified professional psychologist, had never had a client who had gone through the kind of ordeal that I had. The giggling could only have been the result of her fear which made her uncomfortable, a sort of whistling-through-the-graveyard reaction. Only in this case it was more like giggling-through-the-graveyard.

I walked out and never looked back.

This took place about eight months after the fire, and at that point I had completely lost faith in the psychology profession. A couple of years later, toward the latter part of 2005, my experience with the Mad Giggler must have softened because I gave therapy another shot. A friend of mine recommended someone to me, and during our second session the therapist started crying, overwhelmed by my story. That was it for me. I was done with therapy forever. How can these people help me, I wondered. One giggles, one cries. I don't know who needed therapy more, me or them.

The best thing to come out of all this was something that was totally unexpected. I fell in love.

His name is Steve Sherman, and all he did was fix something that forty-nine surgeries, and counting, could not. He mended my broken heart. Somehow, he picked up these shattered pieces and made me truly whole again.

Steve and I met through a mutual friend, Frank Hart, who I got to know first from seeing him at various charity events. Frank wasn't a Station Fire survivor himself, but he was friends with some of the same survivors I had gotten close to. He is a wonderful person who is so easy to be around. We got along well from the start. Our friendship developed, in part, because he really cared. Frank was someone who I could call no matter what and we could discuss anything. Naturally, sometimes the conversation turned to relationships. He was well aware of my fear of meeting someone new. I didn't think anyone would want me and I was convinced that I would never find anyone strong enough or willing to accept me with all this baggage. Then one night Frank called and asked if I would like to meet his friend, Steve, a divorced father of three.

I was terrified just thinking about it. I trusted Frank, and I knew he would only want the best for me, so I asked him what he told his friend about me. He said he told Steve that I was a survivor of The Station Fire and that I had scars. That was it. The rest, he said, was up to me, when and if I felt comfortable. No pressure. He made it a lot easier for me to think about. I figured, Steve already knew about my injuries, and that was the hardest part. And he was still willing to meet me. As difficult as it might be, I thought it would be a good experience for me either way.

Even after I had already decided to meet Steve, I remember asking Frank to tell his friend that I was not looking for anything serious. I threw that caveat out there as a little bit of protection. Frank immediately told me that Steve had already said the same thing to him.

It was on May 26, 2006, when I finally met Steve. He instantly made me feel very comfortable. I told him that I needed to be up front about something and if he wanted out I would understand. I told him that not only do I have the scars on my arms and back, but that my head had been burned to the extent that my hair would never grow again and I would have to wear a wig for the rest of my life. His response was, "So what. I'm going bald, too."

I knew then that he really was OK with everything and that he was someone I could really trust. He made me feel special and I opened up my most personal thoughts and feelings to someone other than my own family for the first time since the fire. He didn't giggle once.

I had said I didn't want to get serious, but I couldn't help it. It was like a dream. It all happened so fast.

We introduced the kids, which was not easy for any of them at first. Steve and I did our best to make them feel more comfortable, and we did this by having them be around one another more, not less. In no time, it all worked out for the best. They get along great. Then, just four months into the relationship, Steve asked me to marry him. We were walking along the beach when he suddenly turned to me and proposed. I'm sure that he had thought about it beforehand, but it seemed as if it had just occurred to him at that very moment. It took me by complete surprise and I admitted that I was a little scared.

"Then I'm not the only one," he said. "We may as well be scared together."

It just felt right. The next word out of my mouth was a very loud and definitive, "YES!"

We got married on May 26, 2007, exactly one year after we first met. Frank was the best man and my sister, Stephanie, was the maid of honor. All of our children were in the wedding party and it was a perfect day.

Of all my many blessings, finding love again in such craziness was the most amazing of all because this was the one thing I had been telling myself would never happen. Like all the doctors who set physical limits for me, I had been wrong for thinking that no one would ever love me after the fire.

The one good thing that resulted from the fire which helped many people was The Station Family Fund. This all-volunteer, nonprofit organization, had been founded by Station Fire survivors and family members and had originally been established to help a survivor who was about to lose her home. TSFF received approval from the IRS to operate as a charitable organization on November 4, 2003, and it has been helping people ever since. Every dollar raised by TSFF goes directly to address the needs of anyone who had been directly affected by what happened on February 20, 2003, including the sixty-four children who had lost one or both of their parents in the fire. Administrative and overhead expenses are paid entirely from donations solicited for this specific purpose. The Station Family Fund also coordinates free legal, financial advisory, and counseling services, as well as helping to identify and access resources which may be available through federal and state agencies or other non-governmental organizations.

What TSFF does above all else is provide immediate short-term financial relief and services, as well as long-term support, serving the needs of the survivors and victims' families that may arise in the future.

Services include assistance with identifying and accessing resources available through federal and state agencies or other non-governmental organizations. They clear a broad path through all the legal paperwork and bureaucracy, which is no small task, I can assure you. They also provide medical co-payments and financial grants on a case by case basis. Financial grants give priority to bridging gaps in care for those who suffered catastrophic injury in the fire. They even arrange for rides to doctors offices.

Grant requests are reviewed by an Outreach Committee, and all decisions are made by a Board of Directors. Priority is determined on the basis of the severity of the disability or impairment and financial hardship. During periods of low funding availability, a moratorium on distributions is placed on all requests.

While several civil judgments have been settled in the wake of the Station Fire, as of this writing no judge has signed off on any of the agreements, so none of the money has been disbursed yet. And it won't be any time soon, either. This is precisely why The Station Family Fund had been established. While individuals in need continue to wait for this money to be released, TSFF is there for us in the mean time. In families with only one income, or having to make due only on earnings from part time work or disability insurance, some months it is difficult for some survivors to pay their utility bills. Because the Station Family Fund was there, the lights remained on for a lot of people.

The Station Family Fund raised and disbursed more than $3 million in private grant money and donations to fire survivors and their families. That sounds like a lot until you divide it by the total number of people who were affected by the fire and the mountain of medical and legal bills that many of them have been left with.

The organization did everything it could, but there is always more that can be done. Depending on the time of the year, the calls for help increase dramatically. In the winter, requests can double because of increased energy consumption and rising costs in fossil fuels and other heating sources. There are other factors that increase demand which are not as obvious. For example, some survivors depend on their growing children for help, but when they get older and go off to college they are not able to be there as much. Also, the money that TSFF takes in each year varies, sometimes widely. People can only give what they can afford in an unstable economy. 2006 was a very rough year, with only $25,000 coming into the Fund. The previous year, by contrast, with the help of a matching pledge from the Alan Shawn Feinstein Foundation, $84,000 was raised. That's a huge difference.

Today, the main business of the TSFF continues to be making psychiatric counseling and medical co-payments, occasionally paying for specialists, as well as helping people with health insurance premiums. If someone's insurance runs out, even if they are eligible for new policies, their fire injuries are considered pre-existing conditions. It's a constant battle.

While programs such as Medicaid and Medicare are a great help, there still hasn't been any direct government assistance for those affected by the Station Fire. This has been an understandable source of frustration for many, especially when it seems that every month some other disaster involving far less consequential loss of life, such as California wildfires, continually inspire large federal aid packages. The Station Family Fund once received a single $1,000 state legislative grant, but that's been it from Big Brother.

So we take care of our own, and will continue to do so. We can only try to do more. Organizing benefit concerts has always been one of the more effective ways of raising national awareness and increasing donations for a cause.

Perhaps the most successful of these events took place around the fifth anniversary of the fire. On February 25, 2008, the Dunkin Donuts Center in Providence hosted the Phoenix Rising concert, as it was called, which featured a mix of country and rock acts. The intention of the organizers was to create broader appeal with music fans, but also to show that this was not just a hair-metal rock problem, but one which all musical acts can relate. Featured acts and artists included John Rich, Dierks Bentley, Gretchen Wilson, Randy Owen, of Alabama, American Idol's Kellie Pickler, Whiskey Falls, Aaron Lewis, Winger, Tesla, Dee Snider and Twisted Sister, Kevin Max, Stryper, Marc Bonilla Carmine

Appice's Tom Scholz and Gary Pihl of Boston, Eric Martin, Danny Seraphine with CTA, Facing Forward, Pete Fish, Travis Davis, Eric Cole, Brandon Allen Read, and Gary Hoey. All the artists performed that night for free. A special thanks should be given to Dee Snider and John Rich, the co-organizers of the show, as well as to Todd King and Telsa drummer, Troy Luccketta, for without them this event would never have gotten off the ground.

Still, the overall involvement of the music industry, which most all of the victims and survivors supported through the years by attending the concerts of their favorite musicians, has been decidedly underwhelming. All the credit in the world has to be given to the acts who gave their time and energy at the 2008 charity concert, as well as the previous events, but the bigger names, such as Bruce Springsteen, have been conspicuously absent from volunteering their celebrity to assist in the cause.

In a subsequent interview, Twisted Sister's Dee Snider confirmed that while big-name performers are usually willing to help once you can get them one-on-one, making that initial contact is nearly impossible.

Snider had once performed at The Station as a solo artist. He recalled the wall-to-wall people and thinking to himself at the time that it was a catastrophe waiting to happen.

Remembering the victims and survivors of The Station Fire is one aspect of a tribute concert, bringing safety awareness to the forefront was another.

"These firetrap clubs are everywhere in the world," Snider said.

This was a statement that no one else in the industry had been willing to say. And it opened a lot of eyes, and wallets.

The 2008 concert was filmed by VH-1 for a one-hour documentary. Approximately $38,000 was collected from individual contributors when the show aired the following month on the music station. A DVD of the event was later made available, but that night the Phoenix Rising Benefit show in Providence raised nearly $300,000.

There were hundreds of people and organizations whose contributions helped to make it the success that it was. Some of the larger donations came in from media conglomerate, Viacom (MTV and VH1), which kicked in $20,000. The Dunkin Donuts Center donated $10,000. John Rich and Gretchen Wilson

Foundation, $12,000. The Barbara Streisand Foundation, $10,000. And so many others.

This was the second such benefit concert organized by Troy Luccketta and Todd King, a board member and former president of The Station Family Fund. The previous one in 2005 raised $100,000 and featured acts such as Telsa, Shinedown and Pat Travers with Carmine Appice.

"When the headlines went away," Snider said, "people thought the problem was fixed. Since nobody else is doing it, we have to take care of our own."

I'd like to personally thank all those individuals and corporations, named and unnamed, who contributed their time and money to the various events and charities through the years to help the people touched by The Station nightclub tragedy.

CHAPTER 19   TRIALS AND TRIBUTES

The first criminal trial to come up was that of Daniel Biechele, Great White's 29-year old tour manager. Of course, it was very highly anticipated by many survivors and the families. The three years since the fire had not diminished any of the emotion and anger that had resulted from Biechele's actions on February 20, 2003. This trial was set to start on May 1, 2006, but Biechele, to everyone's surprise, and against the advice of his own lawyers, pleaded guilty to 100 counts of involuntary manslaughter on February 7. It was a bit of a letdown for everyone, despite the admission of guilt. In a statement, Biechele said his plea was out of an effort and hope to bring some peace to everyone and spare them the anguish of a long, difficult trial. He just wanted it to be over.

At that time, his actual prison sentence had not been definitively determined. Under the plea agreement Biechele reached with prosecutors, he could serve up to 10 years in prison. Despite these sentence recommendations by prosecutors and the suggestions of the defense counsel, Judge Darigan could impose that maximum sentence, but he could also give Biechele a longer term, suspending the time given beyond the ten year maximum agreed upon. It was also within the judge's authority to meter out a lesser sentence if he deemed it appropriate, including one requiring no jail time at all.

Biechele was genuinely contrite and remorseful throughout, and it was difficult in some ways to see a human being so broken and vulnerable in public. It was like watching a man ascend the gallows. I couldn't help but feel for him, despite what he had done. But at the same time, he was not going to be hanged, or lose his life like the one hundred victims of The Station Fire. He was anguished, but so were the many families and fire survivors, so any sympathy for this man was tempered by our own pain.

At Biechele's sentencing hearing in May 2006, I was among those who gave an impact statement during the course of the three-day proceeding. The relatives of close to half of the fire victims spoke or provided written statements which were read to the court by prosecutors. Our instructions were to make statements that were intended for the judge, and to describe how the death of loved ones had affected our lives. We were not supposed to address the defendants directly, or to vent our feelings about the plea arrangement. We were not permitted to show photographs of our loved ones.

Most, but not all, followed those guidelines stipulated by the judge.

With a dozen grief counselors on hand, family members began stepping to the podium, upon which a container of white tea roses rested alongside a box of tissues and a carafe of water. One by one, they memorialized their loved ones and detailed the physical and emotional pain that they continue to suffer due to their absence.

I spoke about losing Fred, and the forty-plus surgeries I had endured so far.

It wasn't out of a desire for revenge or blind hate that many of us wanted to be there to see Biechele punished. Biechele was one of the people responsible for this tragedy, and we owed it to those who had died to be there and give a voice to them.

On May 10, 2006, state prosecutor Randall White asked the court to sentence Biechele to ten years in prison, the maximum allowed by the plea bargain, citing the massive loss of life in The Station Fire and the need to send a message.

Courtroom 12 on the fifth floor of the Licht Judicial Complex in Providence was filled to capacity. Courtrooms 11 and 8 were used to hold the overflow, who watched the proceeding on a large screen video monitor. Local, cable and satellite television networks broadcast the hearing live, including Court TV.

That day, Biechele spoke to the public for the first time since the fire. Choking back tears, he clearly accepted responsibility as well as the consequences of his actions.

"For three years," he told the court, "I've wanted to be able to speak to the people that were affected by this tragedy, but I know that there's nothing that I can say or do that will undo what happened that night.

"Since the fire, I have wanted to tell the victims and their families how truly sorry I am for what happened that night and the part that I had in it. I never wanted anyone to be hurt in any way. I never imagined that anyone ever would be.

"I know how this tragedy has devastated me, but I can only begin to understand what the people who lost loved ones have endured. I don't know that I'll ever forgive myself for what happened that night, so I can't expect anybody else to.

"I can only pray that they understand that I would do anything to undo what happened that night and give them back their loved ones. I'm so sorry for what I have done, and I don't want to cause anyone any more pain. I will never forget that night, and I will never forget the people that were hurt by it. I am so sorry."

Following this, Thomas Briody, Biechele's lawyer, asked the court to sentence his client only to community service, citing that the defendant had no knowledge that the foam was highly flammable and that he did not mean to harm anyone.

That recommendation, I admit, took some of the sympathy out of his client's corner for me. After Biechele had just admitted responsibility for his part in the death of one hundred people, it seemed rather disingenuous that his lawyer would then try to get him off with a slap on the wrist by focusing on what Biechele *didn't* know and *didn't* do instead of what he *did do*. As for intent, that had never been an issue. These were involuntary manslaughter charges, after all.

Briody also thought it advantageous to remind the court that this was Biechele's first criminal offense.

That certainly is one way to look at it, but another way would be to say that these were Biechele's first one hundred offenses. That would more accurate, at least.

Briody didn't seem to be doing his client any favors even early on. Before the plea agreement was reached, the defense attorney had expressed a strong desire to take the case to trial, with the belief that his client would ultimately be acquitted, either at trial or during subsequent appeals based upon what he considered archaic state laws. He cited that Rhode Island had the stiffest maximum penalty (30 years) in the country, by far, for involuntary manslaughter, which was the same a defendant would receive for voluntary manslaughter if a defendant is convicted at trial.

When Judge Darigan sentenced Biechele to fifteen years in prison, with four to serve and eleven years suspended plus three years probation, he remarked, apparently on the tour manager's genuine penitence and sorrow, "The greatest sentence that can be imposed on you has been imposed on you by yourself."

Darigan certainly gave great consideration to Biechele's personal admission of wrongdoing and his sincere desire to make peace with the families by waiving the right to trial and the appeal process.

What this sentence meant was that Biechele would be eligible for parole in September 2007, and evidently this was a perfectly acceptable outcome in the eyes of Judge Darigan, who deemed Biechele as someone who was highly unlikely to re-offend, a judgment that is always a mitigating factor in the court's decision when imposing a sentence upon a guilty offender.

Judge Darigan had no state sentencing benchmarks for involuntary manslaughter to consider, and imposed the sentence on Biechele based largely upon the deal that had been worked out between the A. G.'s office and the defense.

I thought the sentence was not harsh enough. The immediate reaction in the courtroom was mixed. Many were understandably outraged, while others believed the punishment was just in this case.

After the hearing, Judge Darigan left the courtroom through a side door, escorted by a personal entourage of court officers. The need for protection from possible reprisal from unappreciative family members was real. Moments before, just after Biechele was sentenced, several spectators yelled out and cursed Darigan's decision.

Given the deeply personal nature and high level of emotions of this trial, not everyone was going to be satisfied with the outcome. Let's face it, there would be no victory here, regardless of the length of prison time the judge imposed on Biechele. Fred and the ninety-nine others who were lost were never coming back, but if justice in this case was going to start and end with Biechele's sentencing, that was where many of us had the most difficult time digesting the plea agreement that the court accepted and the sentence that was imposed.

After Biechele's trial, it was the Derderians' turn. At least we had that to look forward to. With separate trials scheduled, we would get to see two of the defendants get what was coming to them. Or so we thought.

Like Biechele, the brothers suddenly decided to change their pleas and struck deals that would avert both trials. What appeared to be the Derderians owning up and taking responsibility for their actions was at once something more.

Jeffrey Derderian's trial was supposed to take place first, on October 3, 2006, but as jury selection was underway, a plea deal was struck with both brothers. Judge Darigan told everyone to set aside the date of September 29, for that was when he would officially accept Jeffrey and Michael's withdrawal of "not guilty" pleas in favor of "nolo contendere," which was the equivalent to their admissions of guilt. By accepting responsibility and avoiding the expense and presumably the heartache of criminal trials, their sentences would naturally be reduced.

The families were informed of this development in a September 20th letter from the Department of Attorney General. Patrick Lynch wrote in a clear and strong voice that he objected to Darigan's decision. He expressed the same sentiment in his statements to the public when the news was announced, as if trying to distance himself from any fallout that the plea agreements were certain to generate. Lynch also expressed frustration that he was legally powerless to affect the outcome of this decision, and went on record as saying that he thought the Derderians should both receive jail time, and that Michael Derderian should have gotten more time than Biechele.

I'm not sure how this political doublespeak was received by the general public, but to the families and survivors, the Rhode Island Attorney General's objection was a hollow one. How could it be that the people who his office had deemed responsible for the deaths and life-altering injuries of so many were not going to be brought to justice?

Judge Darigan had also dictated a letter to the families. He wanted us to believe that the plea agreement arranged was the best thing for everyone. He wrote that a trial, "would only serve to further traumatize and victimize not only the loved ones of the deceased and the survivors of this fire, but the general public, as well."

We had also been informed of the sentences that both defendants would receive and the judge made sure it was understood that the different sentences the brothers would receive was a reflection of their respective involvement with the purchase and installation of the flammable foam. He invited the families not only to attend the sentencing hearing, but to address the court and express their feelings about the plea agreement. We had been told that depending upon how much time remained after the victim impact statements had been made, the sentencing would take place on the same day.

This meant that nothing any of the family members said was going to change the sentences, which had already been arranged. Basically, we were just being asked to listen to ourselves talk. Judge Darigan later admitted as much.

"This court has always been acutely aware that no resolution," Darigan said, addressing the court before he imposed the sentences on the two defendants, "either by trial or plea agreement, would ever satisfy anyone or everyone."

The change of plea hearing drew spectators and media from all over the country. When the doors of the Kent County Court House opened at 8:30 the morning of the hearing, courtroom 4E was packed. A group of about 90 people viewed the hearing on video screens in two overflow rooms. The proceedings were televised nationally on Court TV as well as broadcast on local stations and streamed live online.

At 9:30 a.m. the trial began, and immediately after Judge Darigan gave his opening statement, the floor was opened up to the families. Some family members had decided not to speak before the court, believing it was an exercise in futility, and Darigan showed he understood as much when he said, "The court is well aware of the anger, bitterness and disgust. I know there is a feeling of futility."

But I wasn't about to be silenced. I had made a promise to myself that I would keep Fred's memory alive, that he would have a voice through all this, and I was going to speak for him, the same as he would have done for me.

Twenty-five of us had lined up, each given up to five minutes to say our peace. Others had provided the judge with written statements the night before, which were not read in court. Just as in the Biechele sentence hearing, individual stories of heartbreak and loss were recounted, along with a healthy dose of frustration that the case did not go to trial.

It should be noted that there were also family members who agreed with the decision to forgo a trial and believed that the Derderians paid enough of a price. They did not want to publicly relive the night of the fire, and that is something that I can certainly appreciate and respect. But Darigan, as well as the Derderians, seemed to think that they were doing a favor for all of us by accepting the plea agreement and sparing everyone from a difficult and traumatic trial, and this was simply not the case. Many of us were actually looking forward to hearing all the details, no matter how difficult, so that we might gain a better understanding of exactly what happened that night. I felt that this was our last chance for closure and that it had eluded us when this deal with the Derderians was struck. To make matters worse, their sentences were just too lenient.

Some called the sentences mere slaps on the wrist. Others said that they felt betrayed, let down by the system. Unable to repress these feelings, some family members burst out in anger and a few had to be restrained.

"This is not a public hearing," the judge berated the speakers, "it's not a rally, it's not a memorial service and it's not a forum for a diatribe against this criminal justice system." At one point, Judge Darigan threatened to discontinue the reading of impact statements altogether.

"We're conducting these (impact statements) because we're required to by law," he said, "and because we want to hear from you regarding your loved one. I'm not interested in your feelings about the Derderians."

He walked off the bench calling a recess.

When court resumed later that morning, the reading of impact statements was continued. At one point, Jeffrey Derderian openly wept while his defense attorney, Kathleen Hagerty, sat beside him with tears in her eyes. Nearly four hours later, after the last family member spoke, the Derderians were given an opportunity to respond. Jeffrey addressed the court first.

His voice quavering, Jeffrey Derderian began by apologizing. "I certainly know saying that I am sorry isn't enough for people who lost so much. I wish I could give you back what you lost, but I know I can't. I wish I could take away all of your pain, but I know I can't." He broke down as he spoke. "Regarding the foam, I wish we knew how deadly and toxic it really was. I take responsibility for believing it was OK."

Jeffrey said he understood that forfeiting his right for a trial would limit information and facts about the fire. "While we do not have all the answers," he said, "I promise to make myself available to any agency or civil attorney representing victims of the fire and provide all information as best I can."

His lengthy statement continued, and became decidedly cryptic by the end. "There are many days when I wish I didn't make it out of the building," he said, "because if I didn't, maybe some families would feel better. To those families, I'm sorry that I did make it out. I know you would have liked it if I died, too. I hear the screams, the broken glass, the terror from that night in my head."

He pledged that his community service would be taken seriously, and that he would do everything he could to educate people about the harsh lessons he learned about fire safety.

As he spoke, his brother Michael dropped his head on the table, his face grimacing in pain as he sobbed. Later, the older Derderian brother also broke his three-and-half-year silence, speaking publicly for the first time about the fire. He also began with an apology and accepted responsibility for his role in the fire.

"I also want to say that I am sorry for not asking more questions about the deadly and toxic foam that we hung on the walls of our business."

As if trying to justify the installation of the foam, he went on to explain that he was only trying to be a good neighbor by deadening the sound.

"If I had known what that foam was," Michael Derderian told the court that afternoon, "we definitely would have done things differently. We would have never ever put our patrons, our employees, our families and friends at risk."

Like his brother, Michael Derderian also vowed to do all that he could to bring truth and information about the fire out into the open.

"I stand before this court," he said in conclusion, "ready to accept my punishment."

Before imposing the sentences, Darigan took some time explaining the law and why he decided to let the Derderians explain their pleas. Then, after a final request by Assistant Attorney General William Ferland and lead prosecutor for the state to change his mind and sentence both brothers to prison, Darigan said, "The court must sentence the defendants for the crimes to which they have pled, not on the basis of the terrible outcome."

The judge then pronounced that he was sentencing Michael Derderian to fifteen years at the Adult Correctional Institutions, with 4 years to be served in minimum security. The remaining eleven years were suspended, which meant that he may be responsible to serve that part of his sentence in jail if he broke the law again during this time. In addition, he was ordered into a work-release program and serve three years probation after completing his sentence.

You hear fifteen years and, while it was clearly not enough time, you might be initially tricked into thinking that the judge was at least interested in giving him a real hard slap on the wrist. However, this sentence ended up being far more deceptive than it appeared. The truth was, Michael would be released from prison in late June 2009, after serving just two years and nine months. The year before, the Parole Board granted him an early release, setting a date of September 2009. He would have three more months shaved off his time to serve due to good behavior and other favorable considerations.

Jeffrey Derderian's deal was even sweeter, given a 10-year suspended sentence, with three years probation, and five hundred hours of "appropriate" community service, which he eventually completed at a local fire and rescue company and with a national agency that works for burn survivors. The court's thinking behind giving Michael a harsher sentence was due to his direct involvement in purchasing the foam.

Judge Darigan asserted his authority on the matter, telling the court that, "What is important and critical to the process is that this court is the sentencing authority in all criminal cases, and has the right and the final responsibility to impose sentences in these cases."

He spoke these words with more than a dozen security officers flanked around him.

Darigan cited numerous examples which he felt justified the plea change and sentences that were levied against the defendants. These included the length of the trial and the toll that it would take on the families and the 300-plus witnesses who had been subpoenaed to testify. The judge also believed that it would be difficult to seat an objective jury on the case.

The Derderians were initially each charged with 200 counts of involuntary manslaughter, two for each of the 100 people who died. After they changed their pleas, 100 of those counts were dismissed for each brother because the Constitution's double jeopardy clause prevents them from being punished two times for one death.

"Sheriff, you may take custody of the defendant," Darigan said at the conclusion of the hearing, and Michael Derderian was then led out of the courtroom in handcuffs while Jeffrey walked out of the side door of the courtroom accompanied by his family and friends.

It was a long, emotional day for everyone. After the trial, a large group of us remained outside near the front steps of the courthouse, still stunned. A horde of television cameras and photographers stood by the parking garage about 100 yards away. Confronted by the cameras, some survivors and family members stopped and talked to probing reporters. I escaped into the garage.

It was a difficult pill for me to swallow, but this is what they were giving us. After having endured so much over the past three and a half years, accepting this judicial decision should have been a walk in the park.

It wasn't.

CHAPTER 20   LOOSE ENDS

By March, 2007, Alyson Musco, the student nurse who cared for me at Shriners Hospital, had now been a full-time registered nurse for three years. She was still working at Shriners and had married her longtime boyfriend the year before. She was also expecting her first child, and when she learned she was having a girl she paid me the best compliment when she told me she was going to name her daughter after me.

Alyson admitted that both she and her husband had always liked the name Gina, but then after our paths crossed at the hospital and we got to know each other her mind had been made up. Baby Gina was set to make her first appearance in the world at the end of March 2007.

It was during the 4th anniversary of The Station Fire that Alyson reached out to me. She contacted my former case worker to find out how she could get in touch with me, and she did. It was so nice to hear from her and catch up on each other's lives. When she told me that she was due with a little one who was going to share my name I was so happy for her and honored. I couldn't wait to meet my little namesake.

I didn't know how to respond when she told me that she wanted me to know how much it meant to her that her daughter was going to share a name with someone who she felt was the epitome of strength. I was taken by complete surprise. Then she told me that her daughter's middle name was going to be Marie and it was my turn to surprise her when I said, "That's my middle name, too." It was all very uplifting news to hear during a time of the year that I dreaded.

Since that conversation we've stayed in touch, though mostly through e-mail. We made several attempts to get together, but life is hectic, her with a little one and me with a new husband and two growing boys.

In September 2007, the families roundly, though perhaps not unanimously, expressed support of Daniel Biechele when talk of his parole began to surface. In letter after letter to the parole board, the majority favored his release. By this point, with the Derderians being slapped on the wrist and having no public employees held accountable for The Station Fire, many believed that Biechele was being used as a scapegoat in the tragedy. Besides, he was the only one who stood up and took full responsibility for his actions. He accepted his fate and did not try to wiggle out of it. His anguish and regret could hardly be questioned. He did not have to send out personal, handwritten letters to the families of all one hundred Station Fire victims, but he did so having nothing to gain accept the fulfillment of a need he had in his heart to express his sorrow to those who were most affected when he ignited the pyrotechnics that awful night.

Forgiving him, however, did not mean forgetting what had happened, nor did it relinquish the obligation of the court to punish him and *all* those who were culpable for the deaths of those one hundred innocent people. There were bigger fish in the pond of responsibility for February 20, 2003, but state prosecutors never even had their hooks in the water.

On September 19, 2007, the Rhode Island Parole Board announced that Daniel Biechele would be released the following spring after serving less than half of his four-year sentence, citing genuine remorse as well as the support of many family members and survivors.

At the five year anniversary of the fire, at the very site in West Warwick, something quite unexpected happened that really made me think about how everything in life is interconnected. It was during this memorial event in 2008 that I met Grim's father-in-law for the first and only time. This man's daughter was Grim's wife, who was at Shriners when I was there, so my family had interacted with this man in the hospital and later on at various events in this past. This year, my mother pointed him out to me and later introduced us to one another. He was a distinguished older gentleman with kind eyes. I didn't know what to say to him at first, then he suddenly hugged me and began to cry.

I was shocked. I had been thinking that this man had to hate me. Or at least resent me. I didn't have a complex, but just knowing that he had lost a daughter while I had survived the same fire that claimed her, that would have been reason enough. But he wasn't angry with me.

"You don't know what it's like to meet you," he managed to say through fitful sobs. "For me to see that someone had survived the fire, and to look at you now, you're beautiful, you've gotten married and your life is on track. I can't tell you what this means for me."

We talked for a while that day, and he was just such a nice man. I'll never forget him.

"Am I angry that I lost my daughter?" he told me at one point. "Absolutely, I am. But maybe she would not have survived like you did. So maybe God has His reasons for doing the things He did."

I often felt a little anxious around victim's family members, and the belief that they were looking back over their shoulder at me was something that I now realized had all been my imagination. None of them harbored any resentment toward me whatsoever and never made me feel guilty for surviving the fire. Everyone was so nice to me all along. Really amazing. Fred's family in particular, I will be forever grateful. I love them dearly.

On March 19, 2008, Biechele, now 31, was released from jail and given the rest of his life back. He walked out the front door of Rhode Island's minimum security prison at midday. He did not stop to answer questions from reporters as he got into a car that was waiting for him and drove away with his lawyer. I'm sure he couldn't get out of there fast enough, but for many of us it became just a side note. We knew Michael Derderian would be next and then it would be done; some of the guilty would be free and the rest would remain unpunished. According to the law, at that time the social debt would be considered paid in full, atonement for a hundred lost lives.

Biechele had been assigned a parole officer and planned to live in Casselberry, Fla., which was just outside Orlando. He did not respond to any questions from the media.

However, his attorney, Thomas Briody, said in a statement that Biechele would not make any public statements "out of respect for those people most affected by the fire. He was a private citizen before this tragedy, and he wishes to remain so."

The lawyer declined to discuss the future plans of Biechele, who had been married just before reporting to prison.

I was fortunate if for no other reason than I was able to move on. I had more than a semblance of my life back, my job, my children. It wasn't easy, but I had held onto my sanity somehow, as well. I was lucky to have met and married a wonderful man, who made me and my children part of his life and we are all very happy. This was certainly not the way other survivors and family members would describe their post February 20, 2003 lives. Some people needed more, whether it is emotional needs, psychological, financial or medical, but didn't get it. Great strides have been made, but more needs to be done. And more is being done.

With regards to financial restitution, it seemed that every day more money was being thrown at the survivors and the families of the victims to resolve some of these problems. However, it hasn't quite worked out that way yet.

Six years after the fire, a total of $176 million had been amassed for the families by sixty-five defendants in the massive civil settlement. Including among these is American Foam Company, the Johnston, Rhode Island-based company that sold the flammable foam that was being used as soundproofing at The Station. They agreed to pay $6.3 million to settle the lawsuit pending against them, which alleged that they did not warn the nightclub owner that the foam was flammable.

The settlement also covered the estate of Aram Der-Manouelian, the company's former president who has since died, and Barry Warner, a company salesman who lived near the club and suggested that the Derderians buy the foam in order to quell noise complaints they were receiving from neighbors.

American Foam sold the club $575 worth of foam in June 2000, three months after the Derderians bought the nightclub. The foam is commonly known to burn like gasoline, emit dense smoke and toxic gases and is not suitable for acoustic insulation. Although the Derderians had pleaded no contest to 100 counts of involuntary manslaughter charges, that have said they never knew the foam was flammable.

DerManouelian told the grand jury investigating the fire that his company does not provide technical information on the foam it sells unless a customer requests it, amounting to a deadly Don't-Ask-Don't-Tell policy.

Warner verified this practice, saying that he never told the Derderians the foam was flammable, and adding that the brothers never asked.

It was a big circle of incompetence and unaccountability.

American Foam's insurer has offered to pay $5 million, with the corporation responsible for the remaining $1.3 million.

Sealed Air Corporation, a New Jersey company that makes several packaging products, including Bubble Wrap, were also the manufacturers of the foam that was used on the walls to soundproof The Station. They agreed to a $25 million settlement.

In March 2008, JBL Speakers anted up, settling out of court for $815,000. JBL had been accused of using flammable foam inside their speakers. At the same time that the company handed over a check, they denied any wrongdoing.

Anheuser-Busch offered $5 Million. McLaughlin & Moran, their distributer, agreed to distribute $16 million of their own.

In February 2008, Clear Channel Broadcasting, the parent company of WHJY, one of the sponsors of the Great White concert, shelled out $22 million. They said they were not responsible for the fire, but paid out because they wanted to bring closure to the survivors.

Also in February 2008, LIN Broadcasting and WPRI-TV made an out-of-court settlement of $30 million. The Providence television station became part of the civil suit with allegations that Channel 12 cameraman, Brian Butler, paused in an exit to film the fire and prevented some victims from escaping, allegations the station vehemently denied, citing that it was their insurance company that decided to settle the matter with a financial disbursement.

Some companies, including The Home Depot, who even I have difficulty understanding what their exact liability had been, have made unspecified offers. But when all this money will actually get to where it is intended, and what will be left after the lawyer's get through with it is anybody's guess.

Then, in August 2008, the last two major defendants, the town of West Warwick and the State of Rhode Island, to the shock of everyone, announced in federal court filings that they have each agreed to pay victims of The Station Nightclub Fire $10 million in tentative settlement agreements.

"While we know this settlement will never ease the pain of those enduring enormous heartbreak, it does bring years of court proceedings to an end," Rhode Island Attorney General Patrick Lynch said in a statement afterward.

It's hard to fathom how they came up with the figure $10 million, but perhaps they estimated it would have cost them at least that much, maybe more, to litigate the case through the system. It effectively excused them from any further liability, particularly the former West Warwick Fire Marshal, Denis Larocque, who was roundly blamed by the families for failing to cite the club for using cheaper, flammable foam in place of typical soundproofing material despite repeated visits to the building.

They wanted it to appear as if the money was a charitable donation, because neither the state nor the town has admitted any wrongdoing. Lawyers for the families have said all along that the state, through deputy fire marshals like Larocque, was responsible for enforcing building and fire code laws and for proper building inspections.

Larocque, who has never spoken publicly, told investigators that he missed the foam because he had been more focused on a stage door that swung the wrong way and because his inspections looked more into equipment such as emergency lighting and fire extinguishers.

It should be noted that the door, which seemed to have been the primary focus of Larocque's previous three inspections, was never fixed either. No fine was ever imposed for the repeated infraction. No temporary shutdown of the club until it was fixed.

When asked how town inspectors could have repeatedly cited an establishment for the same infraction and not take any action against the club, West Warwick town manager, Wolfgang Bauer, suggested that someone, such as an employee, must have removed the door to comply with the inspection citation, and then went to the trouble of going back to replace it afterward.

If that was so, it fooled Larocque. Talk about a guy who was showing up for work, going through the motions and collecting his check every week. Larocque was the poster child for that. He retired soon after on occupational disability.

Sounds more like occupational inability.

Besides Larocque, the settlement also covered a town police officer who was accused of allowing overcrowding while working security at the club that night and also a town building official blamed for failing to enforce building codes.

The immunity granted to public employees holds that they cannot be criminally responsible unless there is evidence of malice or bad faith.

And that's just plain wrong, in my opinion.

The town of West Warwick, which has been in a fiscal crisis of its own for some time, agreed to borrow whatever portion of the settlement that exceeds its insurance. Complicating the matter, Republican Governor Don Carcieri and the Democratic-dominated General Assembly needed to approve the state's $10 million settlement and any potential borrowing by the town of West Warwick.

When the town of West Warwick proposed their next budget for the upcoming fiscal year, it included a line item for $600,000 to pay the first installment on a 20-year bond issue to cover the town's $10 million share of the fire settlement. The budget had been drafted by the town manager and it was quickly approved by the Town Council.

In September 2008, Great White offered to pay $1 million to settle the federal lawsuit claims against them. This was not Jack Russell's money or the band's. It was the amount of money that was available through their insurance. No other assets were available, so it was the $1 million insurance policy money or nothing.

This tentative settlement agreement, filed in the federal courthouse in Providence, covered the surviving band members, the band manager, Manic Music Management, that company's agent, Paul Woolnough, Daniel Biechele and Great White's record label, Knight Records.

While no criminal charges were made against them, the civil suits against them alleged that the band was negligent in the use, operation, management and installation of the pyrotechnics, which when detonated "caused deaths of and severe personal injuries to plaintiffs." The suits also alleged that the parties failed to exercise reasonable care for the safety of the patrons of the nightclub as well as failing to comply with the Rhode Island Fire Safety Code.

The day the Great White lawyers filed the claim, offering the insurance money, they left the courtroom without any comment to the media.

It was this insurance payout by Great White that brought the final amount of money offered to settle The Station Fire claims to $176 million. Not that this was some kind of telethon tote board we were watching light up, but since none of this money had been dispersed it was always curious the way the press liked to publicize the tally every time a settlement was made. It didn't seem real. It may just as well have been Monopoly money, for all it was worth. Better yet, they could have printed a million dollar bill and put Jack Russell's face on it.

A trust fund had been set up as a depository for all the settlement proceeds, but before any of the monies could be dispersed it needed to be decided who would receive a share and exactly how much each would be awarded. To determine this, Francis McGovern, a Duke University law professor, was appointed by the judge to craft a formula to determine how much money each family should receive.

McGovern's plan operated on a point system, and he proposed different point systems for death cases and for injury claims. The system is similar to those used in other large liability cases, such as the settlements in the 9/11 attacks. As long as plaintiffs could prove they were inside the West Warwick club the night of the fire and could properly document injuries, whether physical or psychological, they would receive a share of the $176 million.

The points were to be allocated by categories of harm, such as a minor losing a parent, medical expenses and physical and psychological injuries. Each category was appointed a set number of points, and each victim would be assigned a point total based on the categories of harm that apply. Points would be awarded for injuries, pain and suffering, permanent disability, scarring, lost earning capacity and lost earnings.

Once all of the plaintiffs have been assigned their points, the total points that all of the victims received would be added together, then this sum would be divided by $176 million to determine a dollar amount for each point. Then, each person's total points would be multiplied by this amount, determining the gross amount that a person would receive, before legal fees and expenses are deducted.

Personal injury lawyers often take 30-40% of settlements or jury awards, though they sometimes agree to take less, as was the case with the special master appointed to oversee distribution of the 9/11 Fund, which was financed by U.S. taxpayers. McGovern has agreed to donate his services to the victims, though his expenses will be deducted from the settlement fund. Other lawyers have not said how much they will charge.

While none of us were given precise figures on what they might actually receive, some victims were told that they could expect to receive several hundred thousand dollars while others may get less than $20,000. A few were expected to receive more than $1 million.

Joe Kinnan, who had been one of the most severely burned survivors, and who had spent a total of 10 months and 17 days in hospitals, was expected to receive the most money. Gina Gauvin, who had been hospitalized for 133 days and had accumulated personal in-patient expenses for hospital care that totaled $450,000, would also have an exceedingly high point total.

Even with this plan in place, it was understood that the victims would not be seeing any money for many months. U.S. District Court Judge Ronald R. Lagueux, who was presiding over this massive tort case, had to approve the final plan of distribution. In addition, approval by all the victims' families was also required. The survivors were required to submit claim forms through their lawyers, with the necessary documentation, to a neutral verification expert who will verify that each completed form is accurate. The neutral expert would be appointed by the court and chosen by the victims' lawyers.

The proposed settlement must also be approved by the bankruptcy court, which has the ability to reduce the amount to pay specified fees and expenses.

In January 2009, the plan to distribute the $176 million was filed in federal court, where it will remain until the disbursement gets final approval. The money, however, only seemed closer to the plaintiffs than it was in reality. There was talk in the press that some of the survivors were about to become instant millionaires, and referred to this expected and sudden wealth as the next burden that those injured in the fire would have to endure. This talk came as the result of a financial planning workshop in May which had been sponsored by The Station Family Fund and the Phoenix Society. The organizations certainly meant well, and important decisions have to be made after any life-changing event, something Station Survivors knows all too well. But we are not

Welfare lottery winners, or down-on-our-luck gamblers who hit a slot machine jackpot. Worrying over how to spend a lot of money may be a problem for some, but it is still a good problem to have.

In September 2009, delays were announced and it was speculated that no money would be disbursed until sometime the following year. So the survivors continue to wait, at least as of this writing, for the disbursement of the settlement money and the *burden* that accompanies it. But when the money does come, which it eventually will, it's not going to make our scars disappear and it's not going to bring back the hundred people who were lost. None of us are going to retire and move to Acapulco. We'll pay off some bills and dig out of some of the debt that has accumulated. A few may even go out and spend some of the money frivolously, but none of us will ever forget.

AFTERWORD

My journey is not over. While my condition continues to improve, even if by smaller and smaller degrees these days, my desire to reach out to other burn victims grows more intense. With increasing physical capacity comes further opportunity for me to help those in need, which I look forward to doing when the occasion should arise.

One such occasion was on October 8, 2008. I had been asked to speak that day at a local Shriners gathering at their headquarters in Cranston, not far from my home. They wanted to hear about the many positive experiences I had, along with my family, during my stay at The Shriners Burns Hospital in Boston. I was more than happy to do it, and there was never any problem with making time available to talk to them, but I was very nervous about speaking in public to strangers. I was probably psyching myself out all that previous week, but then something happened that night when I walked into the reception hall and found myself face to face with around one hundred fifty members of the fraternal organization. I couldn't believe that so many people actually would be interested in anything I had to say. Thinking that way probably made it easier for me when it came my time to speak, because once I got up there in front of them I suddenly felt very at ease.

It was just a perfect opportunity for me to thank them for saving my life, and that's what I did. These were the same people who are responsible for the network of hospitals that does so much for children around the country. They are truly incredible. Everything I said that night I meant. I wasn't just blowing smoke. If speaking about my personal experiences at the hospital were to somehow enhance the growth of this organization and allow them to continue to support the hospitals, then in small way I would be helping.

We got some press coverage and it felt good knowing that it would raise public awareness of Shriners while at the same time giving its members an opportunity to see how their charitable fundraising restores life.

It was a wonderful and fulfilling experience for me, as well, but it left me wanting to do more. I began feeling an inner pull, or a calling, if you will, to do all that I could to get involved in other burn charities and organizations. While The Station Family Fund continues to help families of The Station Fire, one day its mission will be complete. Unfortunately, there will be other fires and families that will be affected by them. I was shocked when I first learned that more than a half million people receive medical treatment each year for burn injuries. I wanted to do something for other people who had gone through the same trauma that I had, and that's how I became interested in working with The Phoenix Society, an organization whose main objective is to ensure that everyone impacted by a burn injury has access to the necessary resources for recovery.

The Society was founded by Alan Breslau, who was extensively burned in the crash of a commercial airliner in 1963. Following a visit to a young boy in a burn center, Alan realized the importance of peer support for those with burn injuries and went on to establish one of the first burn support organizations in the United States. In 1977 Alan Breslau officially incorporated The Phoenix Society For Burn Survivors, Inc., which takes its name from the mythological bird that lives 600-800 years and then is consumed by flame, but rises again, reborn from its ashes, more brilliant than before.

To those of us who have experienced a burn injury or those who have supported us on this road, the transformation of the legendary Phoenix speaks volumes. The Phoenix Society identifies three steps in this transformation process: recover, renew, and return.

For over thirty years Mr. Breslau worked tirelessly to expand the burn survivor network from an office in his home in Levitton, Pennsylvania. Beginning with modest resources and limited staff, he was able to touch thousands of lives and eventually fulfill his dream of serving as a national resource center for burn survivors and those who care for them. He had envisioned a day when every person who experiences a burn injury will not only receive outstanding medical care to physically recover, but will also be supported in his or her emotional and social recovery. They will recover, renew, and return to a meaningful and full life because of the efforts of this community.

Today The Phoenix Society is a leading national nonprofit organization dedicated to empower anyone affected by a burn injury. Their core belief is that support from someone who has truly "been there" can provide the hope needed for recovery of mind, body, and spirit. I certainly had been there, and now I saw an opportunity for me as a volunteer through SOAR (Survivors Offering Assistance in Recovery), which is a program designed by The Phoenix Society and a national committee of experts to provide training to burn survivors or their family members who want to volunteer to help others whose lives have been touched by a burn injury. The hospital-based program is intended to make it easier for burn centers to work with volunteers in providing peer support to patients. Peer support assists individuals in adapting to a burn injury through sharing similar experiences.

The problem was that Rhode Island does not have a SOAR chapter in any of its hospitals, but this is something I am committed to help change. Massachusetts General and Shriners in Boston were the only New England hospitals with a SOAR program.

When SOAR was first introduced in 2001, six hospitals were chosen to implement the program. Soon after, the program proved so successful that there are now more than thirty burn centers in the process of implementing a SOAR program. Many people who successfully recover from a burn injury find purpose and meaning by helping other survivors do the same. Those who recover successfully have learned a lot through trial and error and can make the road easier for others. The SOAR training program also empowers volunteers with information and skills needed to provide appropriate forms of support. I would be appropriately trained, and once a patient or patient's family has been identified as wanting to speak to another burn survivor, the burn center hospital staff would contact the SOAR coordinator who would then arrange to have me, a peer supporter, meet the patient or family. I would be working in a hospital setting as I had always wanted to do, having something to offer and helping people. It was almost as if my life had been scripted precisely to get me to this place in life where I would be doing this very thing. Despite what I had to endure to arrive at this destination, or more properly because of it all, I feel that this was meant to be.

The word "soar" means "to rise, glide or fly in the air, to climb quickly or powerfully." If you were to ask any burn survivor about the meaning of the word "soar," he or she will tell you that air isn't required to soar. All you need to soar is hope, love and the support of loved ones and the community. It is exactly what I found helped me overcome some very long odds on my road to recovery, renewal and return to my life.

Adopting the symbolism of the Phoenix, which I first learned all about only after I began my own journey of recovery, I now have a colorful red and yellow tattoo on my left calf of the legendary winged bird rising from flames.

A song which has become an unofficial anthem for me, and a great source of inspiration, is R. Kelly's "I Believe I Can Fly."

I believe I can fly
I believe I can touch the sky
I think about it every night and day
Spread my wings and fly away
I believe I can soar
I see me running through that open door
I believe I can fly...

It's a beautiful song with such perfectly fitting lyrics that it's hard for me not to liken them to a burn victim's recovery of spirit. People have referred to me as brave and strong, but I've never felt that way. Many times I was just the opposite, lost and afraid. And I did not think I was any stronger than anyone else. My family was my strength, and the courage of all my caregivers is the only reason I'm alive today. But if I could be a source of inspiration to others, through this book or in my deeds in life, then I know I would have achieved something truly great.

Now, seven years later my life continues to move forward. My sons, Alex and Nick, are growing into fine young men. I am grateful for every moment with them and my entire family. I have been asked through the years, "Will you ever get over this?" The answer will always be "No." My scars will always be there, and every time I look in the mirror I am reminded of what happened on February 20, 2003. However, I do not let it slow me down, or keep me from doing the things I can do and enjoying them to the fullest

There is still so much of life left for me to live.

CPSIA information can be obtained at www.ICGtesting.com
Printed in the USA
LVOW01s0708260114

370904LV00012B/329/P